Mommy, I'm Bored

Also published by Cynthia MacGregor

Creative Family Projects, Games, and Activities

Mommy, I'm Bored

127 Fun-Filled and Educational Games Your Child Can Play Alone

Cynthia MacGregor

A Citadel Press Book

PUBLISHED BY CAROL PUBLISHING GROUP

A Citadel Press Book

Published by Carol Publishing Group

Citadel Press is a registered trademark of Carol Communications, Inc.

Editorial Offices: 600 Madison Avenue, New York, N.Y. 10022

Sales and Distribution Offices: 120 Enterprise Avenue, Secaucus, N.J. 07094

In Canada: Canadian Manda Group, One Atlantic Avenue, Suite 105, Toronto, Ontario M6K 3E7

Queries regarding rights and permissions should be addressed to Carol Publishing Group, 600 Madison Avenue, New York. N.Y. 10022

Carol Publishing Group books are available at special discounts for bulk purchases, sales promotion, fund-raising, or educational purposes. Special editions can be created to specifications. For details, contact: Special Sales Department, Carol Publishing Group, 120 Enterprise Avenue, Secaucus, N.J. 07094

Manufactured in the United States of America

10 9 8 7 6 5 4 3 2 1

Library of Congress Cataloging-in-Publication Data

MacGregor, Cynthia.

    Mommy, I'm bored : 127 fun-filled and educational games your child can play alone / Cynthia MacGregor.

    p. cm.

"A Citadel Press book."

ISBN 0-8065-1662-3 (pbk.)

1. Amusements.   2. Games.   3. Creative activities and seat work. I. Title.

GV1203.M32 1995   95-19229

790.1'922—dc20   CIP

For David
With bushels of love

Contents

Acknowledgments • xi
Introduction • xiii

Paper & Pen Pastimes • 1

Author, Author! • 3   Hold the Presses! • 4
Cowboy Poets and the Belle of Amherst • 6
Rock-It Scientists/Un-Rapp-ing Talent • 11   Update a
Fairy Tale • 12   Aesop Revisited • 13   Scrambled
Words • 14   Three-Way Words, Four-Way Words • 15
Add 'n' Change • 16   Hidden Animals • 17   Word
Golf • 19   Word Search • 20   Telephone Words • 20
Pangrammatically Yours • 21   Gorge Washington? • 22
Tough as Nails, Easy as Pie? • 23   Word Marriages • 24
Rebuses • 25   Secret Codes • 26   Gonna Sit Right
Down and Write Myself a Letter • 28   A Letter to
Grandma • 30   A Book of Memories • 30   Lights!
Cameras! Action!–Script First! • 32   Progressive
Alphabet Story • 34

Artistic Adventures • 37

Comic Relief • 39   Sight-Free Drawing • 40
Squiggle Pictures • 40   Mirror, Mirror • 41
Birthday Jigsaw Puzzle Greetings • 41   Blank Jigsaw
Puzzles • 42   Make Simple Collages • 44   Paper
Mosaics • 45   Rice Is Nice for Mosaics • 46

Contents

Make an I-Love-You Present • 47

Even If It Isn't Near Christmas • 48

Make Book on It • 49   Comical Books • 51

Favorite Story in Pictures • 53

Homemade Stationery • 54   Occupied by Design • 55

Home Decorating • 57   Reverse Silhouette Art • 60

Personal Best • 61

Basket Bounce • 63   Boxbaskets • 64

Basketbubbles • 65   TP Bowling • 65   Checker

Chase • 66   Flying Shuffleboard • 67   Slingshot

Buckets • 69   Take Me in to the Ball Game • 70

Sheet Ball • 73   Indoor Mini-Golf • 74

Goofy Golf • 75   Nickel Golf • 76

Solitaires & Similar Solos • 79

Skip Two • 81   Ace-Deuce-Three • 82   Domino

Knockdown • 83   Idiot's Delight (Domino

Survivors) • 84   Solo Concentration • 85

Heads or Tails—What Are the Odds? • 87

Dribbler's Squares • 88   Button Baseball • 91

Skill Builders • 95

Knowledge Challenges • 97   Rolling (in) Wealth • 98

The King Was in His Countinghouse • 99

Just What Is a "Countinghouse"? • 101   Shop 'Till

You Drop • 102   Order in the Court(yard) • 103

X Marks the Spot • 105   Alphabet Book • 107

Contents

Memorizing Instructions • 108
Personal Timelines • 109   Your House Is a Game
Board • 111   Introducing You To… • 114

"Photo Opportunities" • 117

These Balloons Don't Fly • 119   Newspaper
Capers • 120   Homemade Jigsaw Puzzles • 121
Uncle Allan's in Pieces! • 123   Magazine Picture
Scavenger Hunt • 124   Magazine Letter Scavenger
Hunt • 125   Photo Finish • 127   Picturing a
Childhood • 129   Mixed-Media Art • 131   Photo
Collages • 133   The Missing Half • 134   Mixies • 134

Miscellaneous Activities • 137

"Ransom" Stories • 139   Dry-Land Fishing • 140
Friend-Ships • 141   Circus Train • 142
Squirt-a-Cup • 143   How Do You Get to Carnegie
Hall? • 144   Sears, Roebuck, & Annie • 147
Kiddie City • 148   Spool Tool • 151   Grab-Bag
Guessing Game • 152   Football-Card Football • 153
Blockless Building • 154   Ace of Towers • 155
Splish-Splash Bowling • 156   A Button-Down
Mind? • 157   To-Whit-To…Who? • 159   Sit! Heel!
Roll Over! • 160   My Memory Book • 161
Treasure Chest • 164   Be an Inventor • 166
Presenting…Our New DJ! • 166   And Now This
Public Service Message • 167   "I Did Not Say 'Clean
Your Room'" • 168   Rearrange Your Room • 170

Contents

Snow Paintings • 171   Pinfinders, Inc. • 172
The Price Is Right—Right at Home • 175
Good Luck! • 176   Play the Waterphone • 177
Sock It to Me! • 179   And Now a Word *About* Our
Sponsor • 180   Rock Face Paperweights • 182
Work Plans • 182   Birthday Calendar • 185
Paper Dolls • 186   Cardboard Dollhouses • 188
Quickies • 190

acknowledgments

The author gratefully appreciates the contributions of
(in alphabetical order)
Vic Bobb, John Davidson, and Sheryl Pease

introduction

Whether your child is an "only" or one of four, and whether she has lots of friends in the neighborhood or is the only kid on the block, there's going to come a time when she has no one to play with.

In fact, it's probably going to happen often.

Brother and sister are off with friends; two of the kids on the block have the measles and the rest have other plans. Your child's best friend is on a camping trip with his Scout troop...in short, there's no one to play with. And your child doesn't know what to do.

If that's the problem, you're holding the solution. Here's a book full of answers to the dreaded whine, "Mommy, there's no one to play with." Here's a large serving of activities your child can enjoy without friends. A few require some help from you, but most are activities she can get involved in entirely on her own.

Here are word games, art activities, athletic solos, solitaires both with and without cards, creative writing suggestions to occupy lots of time, skill-building games and activities, a slew of things to do with old photos, and a gaggle of miscellaneous activities of many sorts.

Don't bypass a section just because you think, "Lee can't draw a straight line–I'll skip over the art projects," or "Dale isn't much of an athlete–I'll go past the Personal Best section." There are games and activities in every section for kids with abilities at different levels–or with conspicuous inabilities. Do yourself and your child a favor, and don't overlook any sections.

No one to play with? Of course, if he's old enough to read, your child could always curl up with a good book. But if he's not reading yet, is not an avid reader, or wants a more all-involving activity than reading, the absence of friends doesn't mean he has to resign himself to boredom. And having no one to play with doesn't mean there's nothing to do but veg out in front of the boob tube.

So why don't *you* curl up with a book—this one—and look at all the suggestions for activities kids can engage in solo. There are sure to be days when your child has no one to play with. But being alone doesn't have to equate to being lonely and bored...as you'll see on reading this book.

Paper & Pen Pastimes

A picture may indeed be worth a thousand words in many cases, but there are times when only words will do—like in most of the activities in this section. (Pictures come into play in A Letter to Grandma and in Rebuses.)

Some of these activities involve creative writing; others are word games or other forms of play with paper and pen (or pencil). All of them are fun, many of them are sure to appeal to your child, and most will stretch creative "muscles" or exercise brain power. (You may even enjoy some of these activities yourself. Try your hand at Pangrammatically Yours, Word Golf, Add 'n' Change, or Gorge Washington. You might even enjoy the challenge of writing a Progressive Alphabet Story.)

But whether or not you take the time to try, your child will certainly enjoy these activities.

Author, Author!

Materials: Paper and pen or typewriter

You may be harboring a budding writer in your house and not even know it. Has your child ever tried to write a story? A poem? A play?

Don't laugh. It's never too early to start. I was eight or nine when I wrote a "play." It consisted of four scenes of something like four lines each, but it was produced at camp that summer, and boy, was I proud. From there I "graduated" to poems and then stories.

Many kids love to tell stories to their younger siblings, and often these stories are made up, not retellings of oft-told tales. The four-year-old who makes up a story and tells it to his three-year-old sister is, in essence, engaging in story writing.

So suggest to your child that he sit down and get creative with words. He could write a poem (see Cowboy Poets and the Belle of Amherst, page 6), or a screenplay (see Lights! Cameras! Action!—Script First, page 32), but I'm thinking here more of stories, or "books."

If your child is creative with pictures as well as words, he can first write the story, then illustrate it, and finally staple it between two sheets of construction paper. The front cover should be lettered with the title of the book in big letters and "by [child's name]," with perhaps another drawing or even a blurb on the back cover.

If your child's talents are strictly with words, not pictures, it's enough just to write the story without turning it into a homemade book. Or turn it into a book without pictures—after all, not all books are illustrated. He can read the story or book aloud to the family and to friends, save it for posterity, perhaps even get it published if his school has a newspaper or if he belongs to any sort of youth or recreational organization that has a newsletter.

If you happen to have a photocopier at home—and these days, with more and more home offices, more parents than ever do have office equipment of various sorts at home—your child can even run off copies of the book to give to friends.

Hold the Presses!

Materials: Paper and pen or typewriter, photocopier if available

4

Another writing activity your child can get into is putting together a family or kids-in-the-neighborhood "newspaper." The actual publication may just be one sheet front and back, but your child can write up all the newsy tidbits that have happened around your place lately. If you have a photocopier in the house, your child can run off a few copies of the newspaper. Otherwise, she'll just have to circulate the one-and-only copy to all interested would-be readers.

Many kids who haven't the imaginations to make up stories (see "Author, Author!" above) can still write—they are simply nonfiction writers, rather than fiction writers. If they grow up and pursue literary careers, they'll likely be journalists rather than novelists.

If your child chooses to do a kids-on-the-block newspaper, she can write up hot stories with such headlines as BRIAN MURPHY CATCHES FIRST FROG OF SPRING, MELISSA COREY GETS NEW DOLLHOUSE, ANDY WATSON TRIPS ON PAVEMENT CRACK

AND SUFFERS SKINNED KNEE, ANNE MARTIN TO HOSTESS TEA PARTY, and NEW CLUBHOUSE BUILT IN LARGE TREE IN ADAM'S YARD.

Then she can circulate the newspaper to all the kids on the block, or in the neighborhood, who will love reading stories about themselves even if they know all the details already.

If instead she chooses to do a family newspaper, it can simply circulate among parents and siblings or be mailed out to Grandma, Grandpa, and other close relatives. Did Marie do laundry for the first time in her life, wash Dad's underwear in with her new hot-pink blouse, and result in Dad's having hot-pink underwear? There's a story for the front page! Are you planning to build a new addition onto the house? Did you just have the first picnic of spring? Did Bobby get almost all A's on his last report card? Is Grandma coming for a visit? Hold the presses—you've got some great stories for page 1!

If your child can't use a typewriter, she can always publish a handwritten newspaper, but think how much more real it will look if it's typed...and if she can do it on a computer, in two-column format like a professional newsletter, it will have even more of an authentic look about it.

Hint: Even if there's no computer available to your child, if she can use a typewriter and you've got one of those at home, she can still do a two-column format. Either set the margins so she's typing in two columns, or type each column on a separate piece of paper and paste them onto a third sheet before photocopying.

This year the neighborhood, next year a Pulitzer Prize!

5

Cowboy Poets and the Belle of Amherst

Materials: Paper and pen or typewriter

"Poetry? That's for sissies!"

Pure garbage! You don't have to be an Emily Dickinson, Edna St. Vincent Millay, or Sara Teasdale—in other words, a woman—to write poetry. Carl Sandburg was no woman, and in a lighter vein, neither was Ogden Nash. What's more, there are men making names for themselves these days writing the increasingly popular "cowboy poetry." So you can safely suggest that your bored child write a poem, regardless of the child's sex.

There are all kinds of poems, from long, serious narrative poetry to limericks. Poetry doesn't have to be about "mushy stuff" or even serious stuff. How many people over the years have written about their dogs...and even the most macho-hearted boy can relate to that topic! Sandburg is famous for writing about fog creeping in on cat feet; ask your child to write about fog, then have him compare his poem with Sandburg's.

Without weighing your child down with tons of rules, you can explain that one of the most common forms of poetry is a quatrain—four lines to the verse—and that the most common rhyme schemes for a quatrain are referred to as *abab, aabb,* and *abcb.* What does this mean? If you've forgotten your poetry lessons from high school English, I'll give you a short refresher course.

In *abab* poetry, the first and third lines rhyme with each other, and the second and fourth rhyme with each other. A bit of doggerel that kids can relate to, and that utilizes the *abab* rhyme scheme, is:

> I sat
> In a chair.
> But my hat
> Was there.

The *aabb* rhyme scheme has the first two lines rhyming with each other, and the latter two lines rhyming with each other as well:

> I sat
> On my hat.
> It was there
> On the chair.

And in the *abcb* rhyme schemes, only the second and fourth lines rhyme; the other two don't.

> When I sat with a plop
> On the comfy old chair
> I hadn't a clue
> That my hat was there.

Challenge your child to write a poem—any poem, however simple, on any subject. And if he seems to be getting into it, present this further challenge: Do as I've done above, and write about the same thing—whether it's your dog, or sitting on your hat, or fog, or the meanest teacher in school—in each of the three rhyme schemes above, *abab, aabb,* and *abcb*.

Note that there are other rhyme schemes possible as well, including *abba,* forms that involve more than one verse (or stanza), with the rhymes carrying from one verse to the next, and other forms that involve something other than a quatrain. (A quatrain is a verse with four lines in it. Couplets, or two-line verses, are also popular, and then there are tercets, also known as triplets [three lines], cinquains, sestets, septets, and octaves [five through eight lines, respectively]…but don't overload your child with that information unless he's seriously interested in poetry, in which case let him experiment with as many different forms as he'd like to try.)

Another thing your child can play with in poetry is learning the four basic kinds of "feet" in poetry: iambic, trochaic, anapestic, and dactyllic. Just as you can suggest that he write several poems on the same topic in different rhyme schemes, you can suggest he do the same with different kinds of feet.

An iamb, or iambic meter, goes da-DAH. The word "hooray" is an iamb. A trochee, or trochaic meter, goes DAH-da. The word "mother" is a trochee. An anapest, or anapestic meter, goes da-da-DAH. The word "introduce" is an anapest. And a dactyl, or dactyllic meter, goes DAH-da-da. The word "underwear" is a dactyl. Of course, a meter of verse does not have to be composed of one word. "Mother" is a trochee, but so is "watch it."

A good mnemonic for remembering the different kinds of feet is this poem, which I've encountered in several different forms over the years:

> The iamb saunters through my book.
> Trochees rush and tumble.
> While the anapest runs like a hurrying brook,
> Dactyls are stately and classical.

How much of the above information you'll give your budding poet depends on how serious he becomes about poetry. For starters, it's enough to get him writing rhymed verse in any form. (Blank, or unrhymed, verse is another possibility, but isn't what most kids think of when they think of poems.)

Suggest the following topics if your child says, "I don't know what to write about": My Dog, My Best Friend, Springtime, Winter, Summer, Fall, Snow, Rain, Good Smells, Birthdays, Holidays, School, and Vacation. Let your child feel free to write any kind or form of verse he wants, any rhyme scheme.

Another challenge is to present your child with the first line of a poem, and ask him to finish the poem—in as many lines and any rhyme scheme he wants. Here are some first lines to offer your child:

The rain is splashing on the ground.

My dog is brown. His tail is long.

What would you do with a friend like Joe?

I walked in the woods when the sun was bright.

It's nice and warm. Come out and play.

Raindrops make me think of tears.

Why are people sometimes mean?

I went to the circus and saw all the clowns.

That should be enough to get you started. I just want to touch briefly on one other, very popular form of verse, the limerick. Though many famous limericks are bawdy, there are plenty that are suitable for kids. One old standard clean and funny limerick that's been delighting kids for generations is:

> An epicure dining at Crewe
> Found quite a large mouse in the stew.
> Cried the waiter, "Don't shout
> And wave it about
> Or the rest will be wanting one too."

Kids love limericks. They're light, they're funny, they're catchy, they're singsongy. Challenge your child to write a limerick...or several. Many limericks begin "There was" or "There once was," as in "There once was a young man named Bob" or "There was a young girl from New York." But of course, they needn't start that way at all, as witness the mouse-in-the-stew limerick above.

They do, however, always consist of five lines, normally in the rhyme pattern shown above (*aabba*), and usually with the length and meter as shown above:

> Da-DAH-da-da-DAH-da-da-DAH
> Da-DAH-da-da-DAH-da-da-DAH
> Da-DAH-da-da-DAH
> Da-DAH-da-da-DAH
> Da-DAH-da-da-DAH-da-da-DAH

Whatever form of poetry your child gets into—limericks, quatrains, couplets, or otherwise—and whether he writes romantic poetry, cowboy poetry, or some other form, there's some form of rhymed verse to appeal to many kids of both sexes.

Remember, poetry is closely related to song lyrics. And there's nothing unmanly about writing song lyrics. Or poetry either!

Rock-It Scientists/
Un-Rapp-ing Talent
Materials: Paper and pen or typewriter

Closely akin to writing poetry is writing song lyrics, as I just mentioned above. Whether your child is into rock, rap, or even C&W or gospel, it's never too early for a budding songwriter to get on the road to a songwriting career. And even if your child's future lies in being a lawyer, doctor, truck driver, or mail carrier, she can still have fun writing songs.

Writing the lyrics is easier than writing the music, so let's just concentrate on lyrics for now. There are several approaches your child can take. One is to write the words minus the tune. (Another is to come up with a rudimentary tune to go with them.) Yet another approach, and one that will help her get used to the format of a typical song, is to take an existing song, "borrow" the music, and set her own words to it.

I'm not talking about parody—which I'll also get to in a minute. I'm talking about taking a song, borrowing the tune, studying the patterns of it, and writing your own set of lyrics to the existing tune. It's actually a good way to learn some of the basics of lyric-writing.

Then there's rap, for which your child doesn't need to worry about a tune at all. Rap is carried by its rhythm, its beat.

Now let's discuss parody. Parody involves borrowing a tune and writing lyrics to it that often are satirical and relate to the theme of the original song.

Say you live in Pennsylvania, have had a very snowy winter,

11

and when spring finally comes and you think the bad weather is over, you get unremitting rain. A parodist—your child?—might take the tune of "Oklahoma" and write, to the tune of the first two lines,

> Pennsylvania
> Where the snows are followed by the rain

which is a good play on the words of the original song. Keep going from there. Next thing you know, you have a whole song written, a parody. Your child can do it. The results may be amateurish, childish. Don't criticize. She's just getting started. You may be nurturing a budding parodist or satirist, the next generation's Allan Sherman or Mark Russell.

12

But whether your child writes lyrics and music, lyrics without music, rap lyrics, new lyrics to someone else's music, or parody lyrics to existing music, she'll have a good time, exercise those creative muscles...and be so involved she won't notice, for the moment, that there's no one around to play with.

Update a Fairy Tale

Materials: Paper and pen or typewriter, or cassette recorder and tape

For the child who likes to write but can't think what to write about, here's a suggestion: Update a favorite fairy tale. Often a child is a budding author but gets stuck thinking of plots. ("Mom, there's no one to play with." "Well, why don't you write a story?" "Aaaah, I don't know what to write.")

Suggest to that child that he rewrite "Cinderella," setting the story in modern times. Or update "The Three Little Pigs" for the nineties. (Perhaps instead of the house of bricks we'll now find the practical pig living in a condo? Is there a security guard at the front gate? How's the Big Bad Wolf going to get past him?)

Even a child who hasn't previously shown an inclination toward writing may evince an interest in rewriting old and well-known stories; the prospect of changing a familiar story may be less daunting than coming up with a brand-new story idea out of whole cloth.

Who knows...this may be just the push your child needs to start her on the path to a career as a novelist or journalist. You may be grooming the Pulitzer Prize winner of 2025. Or he may develop a love for language that takes him down other paths, as an English teacher or linguist. But even if he winds up an entomologist rather than an etymologist, storytelling is a fun art, and one that may make him more popular with other kids. And writing stories is a great way to spend time when you're alone.

13

Aesop Revisited

Materials: Paper and pen or typewriter

Here's another writing project for the creative child who finds herself looking for something to do that requires only one person. Write a new fable in the mold of Aesop.

Your child has no doubt read some of Aesop's fables, those famous old stories that teach lessons. Whether she's ever consciously dissected the form or not, she's probably familiar with it. Suggest she write a new fable. It could feature animals or people, be set in olden times or modern, but to qualify as a fable, it needs to be fictitious and teach a lesson, or moral. (Your young storywriter may find it's best to decide on the moral of the story first, then write the story.)

She may even take the moral of her own story to heart and learn something beyond the craft of storytelling!

Scrambled Words
Materials: Paper and pen or pencil

Supposedly when things are "in a scramble," you're in a sorry situation. But not all scrambles are negative. Scrambled eggs are good to eat, and scrambled words are good to have fun with. A "serving" of scrambled words will keep a child occupied for a while, as he tries to figure out what "niol" is supposed to be (it's "lion") and how to unscramble "soart" to form a word (it's "roast").

Here are some more scrambled words you can present to your child (with answers in parentheses after the words). Feel free to choose among them, offering only the shorter words to a younger child, or all the words to an older child or a child with a vocabulary and reading level above his age.

lowla	(allow)
stei	(ties or site)
mese	(seem)
noal	(loan)
aldn	(land)
ebcoun	(bounce)
nurs	(runs)
lapec	(place)
moit	(omit)

tixe	(exit)
reif	(fire)
veail	(alive)
dungor	(ground)
chunal	(launch)
obeva	(above)
grith	(right)
blimc	(climb)

If your child does well with these and enjoys them, you can easily scramble some more words appropriate to his reading level and offer them for further fun. You don't need to fry up any bacon with these scrambles, but you are offering your child a serving of vocabulary practice that's educational while it's fun.

Variation: Have the child make up some scrambled words and present them at a later time, to you, to his friends, or to his siblings.

15

Three-Way Words, Four-Way Words
Materials: Paper and pen or pencil

Some words can be scrambled so they form other words, as we've already seen. But there are some words that will yield more than one word when their letters are scrambled. Can your child find all the other words possible by scrambling the real words below? Copy the lists for your child and present them to him or her for starters; if she's good at it and enjoys it, your next challenge to her is to come up with her own three-way words or four-way words from scratch.

Three-Way Words

eat	(ate, tea)
loots	(tools, stool)
mean	(amen, name)
last	(salt, slat)
stew	(wets, west)

Four-Way Words

meats	(steam, mates, teams)
sale	(leas, ales, seal)
arts	(star, rats, tars)
spot	(tops, stop, post)
stone	(tones, notes, steno)
peal	(pale, leap, plea)
veil	(vile, live, evil)

Add 'n' Change
Materials: Paper and pen or pencil

This brainteaser requires that the child add one letter to a word and scramble the letters to form another word. Merely adding a letter without scrambling isn't sufficient (for example, adding a "c" before "limb" to make "climb," adding an "r" after "tea" to make "tear," or adding an "r" before "ate" to make "rate"). The letters need to be scrambled as well.

Start him off with the following list. (One correct answer is provided in parentheses after each word; other correct answers may be possible as well.)

tear   (rates)
loan   (alone)
ate   (neat)
tea   (meat)
rat   (tart)
dined   (indeed)
rent   (enter)
mast   (steam)
mate   (teams)
slot   (stool)
new   (wane)
owl   (slow)
want   (tawny)
wart   (straw)
half   (flash)

If your child enjoys this brainteaser and completes the list above, ask him next to devise his own list of words to be scrambled, as well as coming up with the answers.

Hidden Animals

Materials: Paper and pen or pencil

Help! The animals have escaped from their cages and are hiding. Can your child find them?

You need to prepare for this one by writing out a few sentences that have animals "hidden" in them. The animal name may be part of one word or part of several words, but the letters are all in their correct order. A few such sentences (and the answers) are below. If your child does well with these and enjoys them, you can come up with more on your own. Happy hunting!

The catch on the screen door is stuck.
(The <u>cat</u>ch on the screen door is stuck.)
Do good deeds every day.
(Do <u>good</u> deeds every day.)
Les wants to see you.
(Les <u>want</u>s to see you.)
A pea is very small.
(A <u>pea</u> is very small.)
Am I certain, you ask.
(Am <u>I c</u>ertain, you ask.)
Gee, see what you did now!
(<u>Gee,</u> see what you did now!)
A car attacked me.
(A <u>car </u>attacked me.)
Grab assurances at any cost.
(<u>Grab</u> assurances at any cost.)
Abe, Arthur, and Joe are coming to the party.
(Abe, Arthur, and Joe are coming to the party.)
Cowards seldom fight.
(<u>Cow</u>ards seldom fight.)
Low lying lands are often wet.
(Low <u>lyi</u>ng lands are often wet.)
Give them ink for their pens.
(Give them <u>ink</u> for their pens.)
This is not terrible news.
(This is <u>not</u> terrible news.)
That moo seems loud.
(That <u>moo</u> seems loud.)

Do vehicles all have wheels?
(<u>Do</u> vehicles all have wheels?)
Vic rows in circles.
(Vic <u>rows</u> in circles.)

Your child won't need a gun for this safari. Bring 'em back alive!

Word Golf
Materials: Paper and pen or pencil

In the game of Word Golf, your strokes are taken with a pen, not a golf club, but just as in regular golf, the fewer strokes you take, the better your score. The object of Word Golf is to change one word to another, which is accomplished by changing one letter at a time (without rearranging the order of any of the letters).

For instance, let's change the first word of this game's name to the second word—"word" to "golf." I can think of two ways this can be accomplished, either of which takes four strokes:

   word wood good goof golf *or*
   word wood good gold golf.

Can you turn a "moon" into a "star?" Sure you can:

Moon moan roan roar soar star.

How about "men" into "nun":

Men man ran run nun.

Without giving your child the solutions above, challenge her to turn "word" into "golf," "moon" into "star," and "men" into "nun." See what answers she comes up with. Remember, the fewer strokes, the better. Fore!

Word Search
Materials: Paper and pen or pencil

Another brainteaser consists of giving your child a long word and challenging him to find as many smaller words in it as he can. For instance, what words can he find in the word "category"? I found the following words: cat, gat, gate, gory, gore, core, tore, care, car, yar, grey, gray, trey, tray, tare, rate, crate, grate, crag, rage, race, get, yet, act, ace, toy, Troy, got, get, rot, tor, coy, great, cater, ate, eat, tea, tear, gear, rote, goat, coat, racy, try, Tory, teary, ogre. How many words will your child find?

If he enjoys this brainteaser, present him with a few more. Other good words include "knowledge," "foundation," and "elementary," but don't be limited to just those few. Even words that don't yield as many words within them can still be fun to play around with.

Telephone Words
Materials: Paper and pen or pencil, telephone

Is your child's favorite team the Yankees? YANKEES is also her phone number, if your number happens to be 926-5337. Is she an angler? If your number is 347-4464, it spells FISHING. Just look at the letters and numbers on your phone's buttons; there are three letters associated with every number except 1 and 0, and every letter but "Q" and "Z" is represented. Many phone numbers can be "translated" into words.

If your number begins with a 2, your "phone word" could begin with "A," "B," or "C." Since there are three letter possibilities for every number (except 1 or 0), it takes a little time to figure out possible phone words. But if your child has time on her hands and no one to play with, an activity that might take a while isn't such a bad thing, is it?

Even if your phone number does have a 1 or 0 in it, you might be able to incorporate it into a combination of letters and numbers. The number 969-1969 can be rendered as WOW-1-WOW. And 786-6371 is SUMMER-1.

So let your child get busy "translating" your phone number into words. Is your number 946-6387? I hope your child is a Mets fan—the number "spells" GO METS! Is his name KENNETH? That's 536-6384. CAITLIN is 224-8546. It's fun. It's phone words!

Pangrammatically Yours
Materials: Paper and pen or pencil

Huh? A pangram? Whuzzat? A pangram is simply a sentence that contains every one of the twenty-six letters of the alphabet at least once. The most famous pangram is probably "The quick brown fox jumps over the lazy dog." But, although it contains all twenty-six letters, it repeats several of them. The purest pangram would be one that contains all twenty-six letters once each. Thus far, the only pure pangrams that have been invented are those employing the use of initials, such as "J. V. Schwartz flung D. Q. Pike my box."

Your child probably won't be the one to discover the long-searched-for pure pangram of exactly twenty-six letters, but how close can he come?

Gorge Washington?
Materials: Paper and pen or pencil

Gorge Washington: president who loved to overeat.

Any child old enough to play with words (perhaps age eight and up, depending on the child's facility with words and general sophistication) will enjoy mangling names and coming up with an explanation in apposition to that name, such as the example above.

If wordplay involving "gorge" sounds beyond your child's verbal sophistication, she can still come up with such names as:

Martha Washing-done: First Lady who took in laundry on the side.
Hugs Bunny: affectionate cartoon rabbit.
Rugs Bunny: cartoon carpet-salesman.
Bugs Beanie: cartoon rabbit who wears a silly hat.
Davy Crockpot: chef of the wild frontier.

And the child with a better-developed sense of wordplay might come up with:

George Rosebush: thorny president.
Bread Flintstone: crusty Stone-Age man.
Al Gored: bad-luck toreador.

Al Bore: monotonous vice president.
Pal Gore: friendly vice president.

As the run of Bugs Bunny–inspired names and Al Gore–inspired names above suggests, sometimes one original name offers several possibilities for takeoffs.

Tough as Nails, Easy as Pie?

Materials: Paper and pen or pencil

Personally, I've never found pie to be easy (unless one speaks only of eating it, not baking it!). But the above comparisons are similes, along with "pure as the driven snow," "soft as a kiss," "white like the Arctic," and a host of more imaginative ones that I'm suggesting your child dream up.

Similes (descriptive comparisons involving the words "like" or "as") and metaphors (descriptive comparisons without "like" or "as," e.g. The grass was a soft green carpet.) are not only among a writer's more effective tools but can be the seasoning to give a delicious flavor to anyone's everyday speech. Whether your child has literary aspirations, or he merely wants to liven up his powers of communication, or he simply enjoys a good challenge to the intellect, pose this challenge to him: Ask him to come up with ten (or twenty) good similes or metaphors that haven't been as overworked as "pure as the driven snow."

He may work as hard as a farmer in haying season facing a storm forecast, strain his brain like a teenager perusing a treatise on nuclear physics, and wind up with as unexpected a dose of self-pride as a shy young woman unexpectedly winning her first beauty contest. (See how it's done?)

Word Marriages

Materials: Paper and pen or pencil

How many "word marriages" can your child think of? For a child who enjoys being made to think a little, this challenge will prove to be fun. When I say "word marriages," I'm thinking of go-togethers like cup and saucer, Damon and Pythias, spick and span, assault and battery, Adam and Eve.

Give your child a couple of examples of word marriages, such as those above, then award her five points for every word marriage she can come up with. (Stuck for more examples? Here are a few more: neat and clean, David and Goliath, black and blue, black and white, bow and arrow, ebb and flow, far and wide, fine and dandy, bread and butter, kit and caboodle [*not* "kitten caboodle"], pen and ink, rod and reel, and stars and stripes.)

You can, if you wish, give your child fifteen points for three-word combos such as lock, stock, and barrel.

What's a good score, a score to be praised? That depends entirely on your child's age, how good a student she is, and whether she's better at language than at math or vice-versa. I leave it to you to know when to heap praise. I also leave up to you the decision of whether to offer a tangible reward for getting a certain number of points. Whether or not you offer a reward, you can challenge your child to reach a certain number of points or simply to rack up the best score she can.

Hey, speaking of "rack," there's another one—wrack and ruin. Sugar and spice, coffee and tea, tea and sympathy...stop me before I pair again!

Rebuses

Materials: Paper and pen or pencil

A rebus is a kind of puzzle in which letters, numbers, or simple pictures are used to represent words. The word "why" would become "Y" in a rebus. "I see you" becomes "I C U," and "You are the one for me" can be rendered as "U R the 1 4 me."

When two component parts make up one word, a plus sign is used to join them and show they make up one word, as in "B + 4" ("before"). The word "be" or the prefix "be" can also be represented by a picture of a bee. Similarly, "or" can be shown by a picture of an oar. A picture of a knee followed by " + D" spells the words "need" or "needy."

If your child is no artist, don't worry; he only needs to represent an object crudely, just well enough that it's recognizable.

But there are rebuses involving no pictures. One classic is

YY U R
YY U B
I C U R
YY 4 me

(Too wise you are
Too wise you be
I see you are
too wise for me).

Your child can have a good time devising rebuses to baffle his friends with. Now, while he is alone, is a good time for him to work the rebuses out; later, when he's with his friends, he can present the rebuses to the friends and see if they can work them out.

Secret Codes

Materials: Paper and pen or pencil

It takes at least two people to send coded messages back and forth, but it only takes one to devise a code. If your child would like to play with someone, but no one's around, she can do a little prep work toward having some great fun with one or more friends by working out a secret code with which she and one or more friends can send top-secret messages back and forth.

Most basic codes are substitutions. Either you substitute one letter for another, or a number for a letter. The two easiest codes are as follows:

Simple number substitution: For A write 1, for B write 2, for C write 3, and so forth. The advantage of this code is that it's simple; the recipient almost doesn't need a code key to decipher it. The disadvantage is twofold: First of all, since the code is that simple, anyone intercepting the message can also break the code quickly and decipher the message. And secondly, unless you separate the numbers carefully, 12 (L) and 1 2 (A B), as well as any other combinations in the teens and twenties, look awfully similar, leading to potential confusion.

Simple letter substitution: In the simplest form, A becomes B, B becomes C, C becomes D, and so on till Z becomes A. So "Cat" would become "Dbu," "Gloria is mean" would become "Hmpsjb jt nfbo," and "Let's start a secret club" would become "Mfu't tubsu b tfdsfu dmvc."

Only slightly more complicated is the code in which you jump three or more letters ahead in the alphabet. Now A becomes D, B becomes E, C becomes F, and so on. Not very complicated, but the snoopy sibling (or despised classmate) who intercepts a coded message will have a much harder time figuring it out.

The same can be done with a number code, wherein instead of A being 1, it's 4; instead of B being 2, it's 5.

It's possible to figure out all the above codes without a code key, but to keep it from taking an hour to decipher a simple sentence, it's much quicker if all the parties who will be getting and receiving coded messages have code keys. These code keys spell out the code, either in such a form as A = B, B = C, C = D, or else in two rows of letters, such as:

A B C D E F
B C D E F G

Random codes are much more mystifying. In such a code, there is no particular order in which the letters are substituted. To prepare one of these, your child should first write out the alphabet across a sheet of paper (using more than one line if needed). Then, below each letter, she writes the letter she is assigning to it for the code:

A B C D E F G H I J K L etc.
K X I M P A D T V N E Z etc.

The letters I have chosen above are arbitrary; she could just as easily assign I to A, S to B, or any other arrangement that she wants. The point is simply for her to write all twenty-six letters of the alphabet once, in order, then write all twenty-six again in random spots below the original twenty-six, assigning one letter to each of the original letters to form the code. Then she copies the key once for each friend who will be receiving the coded messages.

Now she's ready for some top-secret fun with one or more friends.

Gonna Sit Right Down and Write Myself a Letter

Materials: Paper and pen or pencil

28

If you talk to yourself, some people say, it means you have money in the bank. But what does it mean when you write letters to yourself?

It means you're keeping a record of your childhood, to share with your adult self.

The child who isn't comfortable keeping a diary or even a journal, either because it requires too much of an ongoing commitment or for whatever other reason, may still be comfortable with a one-shot letter. Whether he starts the letter, "Dear Me," "Dear Self," "Dear Grown-up Jim," or some other way, or omits the salutation altogether, the premise is that he's writing a letter to his grown-up self, to be opened and read at age eighteen (or on graduation from high school, or college, or at some other predetermined time that marks a passage from childhood to adulthood).

The idea is for the child to describe to his future self the events—highlights and low points, excitements and adventures—of the year just passed, or the year in progress (school year or calendar year), or even his whole childhood to date.

The essay test he aced may seem so important now that he thinks he'll always remember the elation when the teacher handed it back; yet at age eighteen, the memory may be blurred at best, if not gone altogether. The fun when Dad hit the clown's nose at the carnival booth to win a prize, and the clown splashed water at Dad, may cause irrepressible giggles now but be forgotten by age twenty-one. That kiss, playing Spin the Bottle. That home run on the very first day of Little League.

All are fodder for a letter from and to your child; all are memories he needs to hold fast. Even if, in later years, he remembers the incident fuzzily, he'll lose the clarity of the moment and the emotions that attached themselves to the happening. The more he jots down now, the clearer the moment will be later. Memories, events, feelings, hopes, and wishes...all are suited for inclusion in the letter. And even if he writes only bare-bones facts, devoid of feelings, reading the mere facts should bring back some of the accompanying feelings, however many years later.

So ask your child to sit down and write a letter to himself the next time he has no one to play with and is bored. Suggest he seal it, keeping it that way till he's eighteen or twenty-one, or graduates high school or college.

He can't imagine, now, how meaningful that letter is likely to be when opened. But you can. And you might be able to make a believer of your child. So make the suggestion soon.

29

A Letter to Grandma
Materials: Paper and pen or pencil; optional: crayons

The next time your child complains there's no one to play with, suggest that instead of thinking in terms of playing, she undertake an activity that's even more meaningful and can be just as pleasurable…a letter to Grandma or Grandpa or both.

Wouldn't Grandma and Grandpa love to hear from your child? Wouldn't they love a recounting of her recent activities? (If she says, "I don't know what to tell them," suggest she tell in detail about some things she was recently involved in, naming the various activities if need be: "Tell about the fight you settled peacefully. Tell about the B + you got on your story. Tell about the principal falling off her chair during assembly. Tell about the new computer game you got. Tell about your new friend. Tell about our plans to go to Disney World next year.")

She can even illlustrate the letter, with pen or crayons, drawing pictures of some of the events she's telling about. Won't Grandma and Grandpa be pleased to get that!

A Book of Memories
Materials: Blank book, pen

Though most boys look down on diaries as "girl stuff," there's no denying that many famous writers, among others, kept journals, and that many of these journal keepers were men. By referring to a journal, not a diary, you may make keeping it acceptable to a child who would balk at the word "diary." And in fact I'm not suggesting a book about who's the cutest, or who has a crush on whom (though there's certainly a place for such information if the recorder of the journal wishes to include it). I'm suggesting a book that records both the important mile markers of childhood and the day-to-day trivia that is what, after all, makes up the warp and woof of our childhoods.

The word "journal" comes from the French word for "daily," and many people do keep journals on a daily basis. But for the child with too little to report, or so much to report that he's too busy doing it and has no time to do the reporting, there's no law against keeping it weekly.

Many writers keep journals as an exercise in writing, and of course, if the child writes in flowing prose, or attempts to learn to do so, he's accomplishing two purposes at once with his journal keeping. But the child who doesn't give a hoot for good writing can still be encouraged to keep a journal even if the entries in it lack any writing style and aren't even all complete sentences:

"Monday. A in Science test, C in writing test. Kenny in trouble with Ms. Wood for teasing Ellen. Lunch pizza. Cold. Ugh. Rained for gym. No football, calisthenics. Dad started new job. Hope he's home more. Broccoli for dinner. Ugh again." It's not exactly the kind of prose that wins the Nobel Prize for Literature, but it does get the basic info across. And years later, when he leafs back through the book, it will bring back memories.

If the journal keeper does get into his thoughts, hopes, dreams, aspirations, successes, disappointments, wishes, times of calm and periods of inner turmoil, so much the better. A measured amount of introspection, and getting in touch with one's feelings, is certainly to be desired. But if not, at least you have, as Sergeant Friday used to say, "just the facts."

The ideal, then, is daily entries, flowing writing, and some in-depth soul-searching. But weekly entries, jotted notes, and bare facts still serve their purpose. They provide a map back through the winding roads of your child's young years, a map he can retrace from the vantage point of his teen years or his adulthood.

Lights! Cameras! Action!—
Script First!

Materials: Paper and pen or typewriter

32

Small groups of kids—or families—can have a great time making movies for fun. If a child is old enough to treat a camcorder respectfully, she can film a video that will be fun to make and fun to watch over and over afterward. But nobody wants to watch a movie with three kids just waving and yelling "Hi, Mom!" Some kind of story line or outline of action is needed.

You can't make the movie without a group of people to help you, but it only takes one person to write a script.

The child who has no one to play with can resolve her boredom by writing a script for a future home movie—and the prospect of actually making the movie, with family or friends at a later date, will contribute to the child's enjoyment while writing the script.

First she needs to decide if she's going to write a purely fictitious script or nonfiction. If fiction, she can create a completely new story or write her own version of a well-known existing story. Nonfiction topics range from biographies of famous people to slices of family life or life in her circle of friends.

A slice-of-life movie may not need a formal, line-for-line script but will still need some sort of plan. A story, whether it's *Cinderella,* the biography of JFK, or the story of how the family's ancestors arrived in America, should have a script.

Your young scriptwriter needs to keep in mind the technical and budgetary limitations on the film, and the ability of available local talent to memorize lines and to act. If your scriptwriter is a ten-year-old whose movie's actors are going to be her ten-year-old best buddy and her seven-year-old brother, she'd better not give them a 100-page script to memorize!

Never mind if the scriptwriter in your family doesn't know the proper format for a screenplay. She's not planning on submitting it to a Hollywood studio! And I'm sure the actors who will be involved in the project don't know the proper format either. All she needs is to show who's speaking, follow that with their lines, and indicate any accompanying action as well as any necessary sound effects, keeping sound effects to a bare minimum and avoiding special effects altogether.

Your child can have a ball just writing the script...and think, when the script's finished and ready to be filmed, the fun's only starting!

Progressive Alphabet Story

Materials: Paper and pen or pencil

For the creative child who enjoys writing, here's a challenge that will really take his concentration: Write a story in which the first word of the first sentence begins with the letter "A," the first word of the second sentence begins with "B," the first word of the third sentence with "C," and so forth, till you reach "Z."

The first sentence should be fairly easy, as you can begin with "A" or "An." "A boy named Joey had a pet dog named Snarfle." "An elephant escaped from the circus one day." (It is not *necessary* to begin with "A" or "An," however.) After that it will get harder. And by the time the child gets to "X," he may be ready to give up. In fact, if he gets that far, he should be greatly praised, even if he can't finish through "Z."

Nobody should be looking for the child to produce great literature within the constraints of this format. The sentences may be unusually short and choppy, even for a child. But it's a fun challenge, and for the child who likes to write, it's a great way to pass a period of time.

After all, kids like challenges. By the way, older kids like to get in on this one too. Come on, give it a try. Do it today. Easy? no, but it's fun. Fun? Great fun. (Have a try at it yourself.) I've been doing it in this paragraph, in case you didn't notice. Just look— I've done ten sentences in alphabetic order already. Kudos to your child if he can get this far. Laughing at my efforts? Maybe so, but it's fun. No, you don't think so? Oh, come on—give it a try. Perhaps you haven't got enough faith in yourself. Quite an accomplishment if you can get all the way to "Z." Really, your child will enjoy this. So what are you waiting for? Try it yourself if you don't believe me. Under no circumstances, though, should you be critical if your child quits before twenty-six sentences. Very few kids will get all the way through. Why not at least try it, though? Xplore the possibilities. You can do it. Zounds—I've done it (with a little bit of cheating in the "X" sentence).

Your child, of course, will probably want to write a fictional story, rather than what I've done, but you get the idea.

Artistic Adventures

*Y*our child doesn't have to be a junior Rembrandt to enjoy the activities in this section. Crafts as well as art are represented here, and even several of the activities involving drawing are suited to those who "can't draw a straight line." Ever make Squiggle Pictures? Ever draw with your eyes closed? No artistic talent is needed, I promise you.

Your child will stop whining that he has no one to play with if you'll offer him a suggestion from this section. No child can pout for long when faced with this array of activities.

Comic Relief

Materials: Pen and paper (construction paper or typing paper)

If your child is into reading comic books—and what kid isn't?—she'll probably get a kick out of drawing one herself. It doesn't have to be as long as a comic book bought in a store (although if she wants to draw pages and pages of panels, let her, by all means). It can be just the four sides of an 8½-by-11-inch sheet of paper, folded in half from top to bottom and then turned sideways to open like a book.

She needs to decide on one or more main characters and a plot line before beginning to do any actual drawing. She also needs to decide whether to do an "action" comic (à la X-Men) or a humorous story line (in the Archie vein). It could even be a story about your family—either humorous or factual. The comic strip might be a good venue for a wry look at family life. Or she could take a straightforward pictorial look at Great-Great-Grandma's arrival from the Old Country.

And speaking of historical matters, your child may want to draw a comic to illustrate great stories out of history. From the first man on the moon to the *Challenger* disaster, from Washington's inauguration to JFK's assassination, there are plenty of stories in the nation's history that capture kids' imaginations. And it's not just America's history…your child may want to illustrate something out of world history. Or the Bible. Or her favorite story.

Get ready to draw, pardner!

Sight-Free Drawing
Materials: Paper and pen or pencil or crayon

Every kid loves to draw, but sometimes it isn't enough to suggest, "Sit down and draw me a nice picture if you can't think of anything to do." Sometimes the response is the dreaded "Idonwanna." But give your child a different challenge, and somehow, suddenly, drawing isn't just drawing anymore.

Challenge him to draw with his eyes closed.

Give him a piece of paper and a drawing implement—pen, pencil, or crayon—and suggest he draw a house, a dog, a cat, or a person. Whether you literally blindfold him or merely ask your child to keep his eyes closed—no cheating, now!—is up to you. But be sure he can't see and agrees not to peek.

He can turn out several of these "sight-free drawings" if he wants. The results are likely to be quite comical! (They may, on a more serious note, give him a bit of a peek into what it's like to be truly sightless, too, and infuse him with a touch more compassion for those who truly *can't* see.)

Squiggle Pictures
Materials: Pencil, paper, crayons or colored markers

Silly art can be fun! All your child needs to do to make Squiggle Pictures is to hold a pencil, close her eyes, and scribble four or five times on a piece of paper, without looking at the results. The lines should be squiggly, not straight, preferably involving loops, whorls, and curves. Presumably the lines will intersect in any number of places.

40

Then she opens her eyes, looks at the results, and goes to work with crayons or markers, coloring in the enclosed areas made by the intersections of the loops and lines.

Presto! Squiggle Pictures.

Mirror, Mirror

Materials: Pen or pencil or crayons, paper, large hand mirror

Here's a fun activity involving a mirror but no wicked queen or poisoned apple. Give your child a large hand mirror, paper, and something to draw with—pen, pencil, or crayons are more appropriate than anything as messy as paints. Have the child hold the mirror in his nonwriting hand, then look only into the mirror as he tries to draw a picture.

Not as easy as it sounds, is it? But it's fun!

41

Birthday Jigsaw Puzzle Greetings

Materials: Construction paper, crayons or paints, scissors

Does your child have a friend or relative whose birthday is coming up? Suggest she make a birthday jigsaw puzzle for that person. On a sheet of white or pale-colored construction paper, she writes "Happy Birthday _____" (fill in name of recipient) and then draws or paints a picture.

The picture can be suitably birthday-themed, such as a cake with candles or a group of happy kids playing, or two or three presents festively gift-wrapped. Or it might be something that reflects the interests of the recipient. If the card is for Grandpa, a fishing enthusiast, the picture might be a mighty fish hooked on a bending rod. If the card is for Aunt Edith, who has four cats, the picture could be of a kitty. An all-purpose picture will do too.

Your child should sign her name near the bottom. And if she wants to add any further birthday greetings, they would certainly be suitable: "Hope you have a happy day," or "Best wishes for a great year," or anything else she wants to say.

Now she cuts the paper into any number of pieces—not too many or too small, but enough to make it interesting. Just how many pieces that actually is will depend on the age of the recipient and his ability to deal with puzzles. The pieces should, as much as possible, have interlocking bumps and curves, in the manner of a jigsaw puzzle, rather than their being all squares or rectangles.

When the pieces are all cut apart, they can be put in an envelope and addressed to the recipient. Your child may want to mark the envelope, "A Birthday Jigsaw Puzzle Greeting for _____," so the recipient has no question what he's holding or what he's to do with it.

Blank Jigsaw Puzzles

Materials: Cardboard, scissors, pencils, paints (or crayons, but paints are preferable)

There are two clues to figuring out every jigsaw puzzle: the way the cutouts seem to fit together, and the picture that is slowly evolving. But what if there were no picture? What if you were staring at a solid rectangle of green, blue, lilac, red, or some other color? Then you'd have only the intricate shape of the interlocks to give you a clue as to what fits where...and you'd have a much more complicated puzzle indeed.

And that's just what your child is going to have when he makes one of these little dillies I'm suggesting.

He starts with a piece of cardboard, an old file folder, or something similar. You want something that's heavy enough to endure through a reasonable number of uses but is not so thick that attempts to cut it will result in your child's demonstrating the cuss words he's learned from his friends.

The first thing he needs to do is paint one side of the cardboard a solid color. This isn't just to make it more appealing through making the dull cardboard colorful. If the pieces were the same color on both sides, you'd be in an awful pickle. Which side is which? Does it go *that* way or *this* way? By painting one side, your child has no question which side is up. The colored side is up; the gray side is down.

43

A crayon can be used for coloring in lieu of paint, but paint is easier to use for a uniform solid color. If the paint doesn't dry quickly, he may have to put the colored cardboard aside, read a book for a while, then return to the cardboard for the line-drawing and cutting.

Now, on the unpainted side, your child draws a pattern of lines he'll cut along when he's satisfied with them. (Or, again, you [or he, if he's old enough] can cut out freehand if you're brave and daring.) Knowing the level of jigsaw-puzzle-solving he's accustomed to, but taking into consideration that this puzzle will be harder to solve, without a picture on it, the child draws swoops, circles, zigzags, protrusions, and whatever other kinds of configurations he wants for the cut lines.

When he's satisfied that the pencil lines accurately represent the cut lines he wants, someone, you or he, takes scissors in hand and cuts along the lines.

Making the jigsaw puzzle is likely to take up a large enough block of time that there won't be time to try to put it together again, unless we're talking about filling a whole Saturday afternoon. Otherwise, the child is likely to find that it's dinnertime or bedtime, whatever activity is coming up next, by the time the pieces are all cut apart.

But now he can look forward to trying to put the puzzle together again the next time there's no one to play with!

44

Make Simple Collages

Materials: Glue or paste, scissors, construction paper, pictures cut from magazines

A satisfying art project that your child can easily make is a simple collage. In the rock-bottom-simplest form, all that's needed is to cut out a variety of pictures from magazines, then paste them onto a piece of construction paper (either black or a light color is preferable to an intense color, so the background doesn't fight with the photos). Parts of some of the photos should be artfully overlapped over other photos.

If your child wishes, she can cut small pieces of construction paper into strips or shapes (circles, squares, triangles, crescents, oblongs, stars, and free-form shapes are all possibilities). These can be integrated into the collage, pasted next to, between, or partially overlapping the photos.

If she wants, your child can cut out a "frame" of brown

construction paper and paste it around the collage for a neat
finishing touch.

Paper Mosaics

**Materials: Construction paper or other paper of various
colors, glue, one sheet of white or black construction
paper for each mosaic**

To make this attractive art project, the child tears different-
colored pieces of construction paper (or other paper) into small
pieces, keeping each color in a separate pile or plastic bag. Then
he glues each little piece of paper, one at a time, onto a large
sheet of construction paper, preferably black or white, until
nearly the whole sheet is covered with glued-on pieces of colored
paper.

He can, of course, draw a picture in pencil first, then fill in
the lines with colored paper, creating a specific picture of
something. But a mosaic need not represent a tree, a meadow, a
sunrise, or a house. Some of the prettiest mosaics are abstract,
and your child can "wing it," improvising the art as he goes,
pasting down the bits of paper without trying to make them
look like something in particular.

If he wants to frame the picture, he can cut out a "frame" of
construction paper, preferably but not necessarily brown (wood
color), and paste it around the edges of the picture.

45

Rice Is Nice for Mosaics

Materials: Rice, food coloring, paper towels, four plastic bags, paper, pencil, glue

Your child can make rice mosaics easily, and they're fun. The finished product is unusual and attractive. Here's how she proceeds:

Place a few drops of food coloring and a small quantity of rice in each of four plastic bags (one for each color). Shake the rice in the bag vigorously till the rice is coated with the food coloring, then dry the rice on paper towels. Let it dry for about forty-five minutes.

46

While it's drying, draw a simple picture on paper. When the rice is dry, spread glue in one section of the picture at a time, applying rice to each section after applying the glue. The result will be a textured mosaic.

You can keep each section of the picture a different color, or you can mix colors within each section, depending on your tastes and on the nature of the picture, which can be either a picture of a recognizable object or scene, or else an abstract picture.

Make an I-Love-You Present

Materials: Depends on project

Got a bored kid on your hands? If he's got no one to play with, he might turn his attention to making a present for a family member or friend. "But it's not Christmas. Nobody has a birthday coming up." Is that the problem? No problem! My own grandmother taught me years ago that the best reason for giving someone a present is that you were thinking of that person.

Maybe you were in a store and saw something you knew your mother, daughter, friend, or someone else special to you would just love. Or maybe you thought of something you could make for someone that they would really appreciate. Buy that present. Make that gift. Show that person you were thinking about him or her. Show Mom you care about her enough to buy the vase you know would look perfect on the end table or make the bookmark that big brother, off in college, is bound to need with all his studies.

If your child is stumped for what to do when no one's around to play with, suggest he make an I-love-you or friendship present for a relative, a friend, or even a teacher. I-love-you presents (under whatever name) are the best kind, because they show that the giver was thinking of the recipient even though it isn't a special occasion. And every child can make *something,* even if he's not the most artistically oriented. If beaded jewelry is beyond your child's abilities, surely a bookmark isn't.

Has Grandma gotten anything from her grandson or grand-daughter lately? Whether she lives across the street or across the country, surely she'd love to get a pot holder or a felt eyeglass case.

And of course, besides occupying a bored child, this project teaches the joy of giving.

Even If It Isn't Near Christmas

Materials: Construction paper, crayons or paints, possibly glitter or other adornments for the cards

I don't wait for imminent birthdays to buy birthday cards. I keep an assorted supply of the cards on hand, and when somebody's birthday sneaks up on me unaware, or when I realize well in advance but I don't have a chance to get to the store, I'm not in trouble. I just open my drawer, look through the selection of cards, and pick out one that's suited to the person whose birthday I want to acknowledge.

Your child can do the same…with homemade cards.

Many kids make birthday and Christmas cards out of construction paper. But they usually wait till the last minute, creating the cards on the eve of the birthday or two days before Christmas. Often they're in a hurry and would rather be out playing ball, sledding, or building snowmen than making a birthday card for Grandma or Christmas cards for ten friends and relatives.

What I'm suggesting is that, when a child finds herself with some "downtime," a block of time with no homework that needs to be done and no one available to play with, she utilize that time to make a few birthday or Christmas (or other occasion) cards in advance.

She should think of the friends and relatives whom she's likely to want to send or give cards to in the next few months, or even the next year, then sit down and craft some cards.

For the youngest set, a simple crayons-and-construction-paper card is fine. Somewhat older kids may wish to use paint, or to get even more elaborate, involving glitter, yarn, paper lace (such as from paper doilies), ribbons, or other materials. Older kids may also wish to write a brief verse or some other greeting more involved than simply "Happy Birthday," "Merry Christmas," "Happy Hanukkah," "Happy New Year," or another special-occasion greeting.

Cards can be made general purpose or with a specific recipient in mind—friends, relatives, the next-door neighbor who bakes those scrumptious chocolate chip cookies and always includes a half dozen for your child, a favorite teacher, or anyone else your child wishes to remember.

49

Cards don't even have to be for a special occasion. Even commercial greeting card companies today feature lines described as "Thinking of You," "Friendship," and "Love." Think how thrilled Grandma would be to get a handmade greeting card that says, "Just to Say 'I Love You, Grandma'" when it isn't even her birthday or a holiday.

Make Book on It

Materials: Construction paper, crayons or paints, scissors

Got a book? You can bank on the fact that at some time, somebody's going to want to borrow it. Another thing you can bet on is that if you lend out your books, your chances are excellent of some of them disappearing. I'm not accusing people of willfully appropriating what's not theirs…although we all know there are some people like that…but sometimes people forget to return borrowed materials, whether it's a book or a screwdriver that was borrowed, a child or an adult who borrowed it.

Sometimes the borrower genuinely forgets that the item was borrowed. Or he may remember that the item was not originally his, but he forgets whom he owes it back to. Then there's the borrower who remembers the item isn't his, remembers whose the item is, but gets embarrassed over having it too long and is ashamed to return it.

What all these people need is a reminder.

Enter the bookplate.

50

When I was a kid, my family had bookplates with a picture of a stag and the inscription *Ex libris the Aronsons.* I didn't know what connection a stag had to a book, hadn't a clue how to translate *ex libris,* but I knew the broad meaning of that bookplate was "This is our book and if you borrow it you'd better return it."

Your child can take pride in possession of his books, and bookplates foster that feeling. (And if he's proud of his books, he's more likely to read them, right?) I'm not suggesting he order one hundred labels with *Ex libris* on them. I *am* suggesting he make bookplates with his name on them.

All he needs to do is cut squares or rectangles out of construction paper, write some identifying information on them, decorate them, and paste them in his books. How large should each bookplate be? Obviously, the smaller they are, the more bookplates he can get out of each piece of paper.

A good plan is to cut a piece of construction paper down the middle along the longer axis, then cut each of the resultant two long strips into thirds. But don't feel compelled to stick to that size; if your child wants larger or smaller bookplates, that's fine.

The only rule is that the bookplates be large enough to print his name on and yet no larger than the inside front cover of the book.

Once the bookplate is cut out, he prints his name on it, possibly following such words as "This book belongs to" (it could as easily be "Property of" or "This book is the property of"). Then, if he wishes, he can decorate the bookplate with a simple design—a dinosaur, flowers, a sunrise, a decorative version of his initials...whatever takes his fancy and is within his artistic capabilities.

A bit of glue or paste, and the bookplate is affixed to the inside front cover of a book...and he can go on to making another bookplate.

If he owns a decent-sized collection of books, he won't want to attempt to make bookplates for all of them at once; that will make this project seem more of a chore than fun. Suggest he do a few at a time, whenever he's got free time, there's no one around to play with, and nothing else suggests itself as a fun project.

Now if he loans his books out, they're more likely to find their way home. And with increased pride in ownership, your child may even read a little more often himself.

Comical Books

Materials: Construction paper, pen, magazines, scissors, glue or paste, stapler or other fastener

A picture is worth a thousand words. But what if you have both pictures and words...and they don't agree with each other? Sometimes when pictures and words are in direct contrast to each other, the results can be comical.

That's the premise of comical books. The topics they cover can be your own family, world history, current events, or anything else that strikes your fancy. The words will briefly state one thing; the picture chosen to illustrate them will depict something rather contrary, and rather amusing.

Say the subject is last summer's family vacation. Your child might start by writing, near the bottom of a piece of construction paper, "The family's summer vacation, a cross-country drive, got off to an easy start." On the page, he can paste or glue a picture cut out from a magazine that shows something counter to what the words say, such as a picture of a man jacking up a car to change a flat.

On the next page, he might write, "Miles and miles of gleaming highway stretched out before us," or "We were determined that nothing would stop us from having a carefree two weeks." The picture to accompany that might be of a miles-long bumper-to-bumper traffic tie-up.

If, in a magazine, your child finds a picture of a dilapidated shack, he might cut it out and paste it on a page captioned, "We stayed in only the most deluxe accommodations," or "Dad always found interesting places for us to spend the night."

If a picture in one of the magazines shows litter by the side of the road, your child can clip it out and paste it in the book, captioned, "During our trip we saw many fascinating sights." A picture of a scowling man with a shotgun might inspire such a caption as, "The people we met were all friendly and welcomed us." A plateful of food of dubious character might suggest, "We feasted on delicious food throughout our trip."

There are two ways to attack this project: thinking of the captions first, or finding the pictures first. If thinking of the captions first, the child needs to come up with suitable pictures, which in some cases won't be available. If finding the pictures first, he needs to think of a theme that will tie them all together. (Or perhaps he can work on several comical books at once, one about school, one about the family's new house, and one about the environment.)

The more magazines your child has on hand to cut up, the better the potential for finding lots of photos that have great gag potential and of finding suitable pictures to illustrate specific captions.

Favorite Story in Pictures

Materials: Paper, crayons or paints

"Mommy, I'm bored. There's no one to play with."

"Why don't you draw me a nice picture?"

"Aaaah, Idonwanna draw. I don't know what to draw."

Why doesn't he illustrate his favorite story? Suggest he take crayons or paints and begin drawing pictures to illustrate his favorite book or story. Whether it's *Cinderella, Alice in Wonderland*, some other classic, or a more modern favorite, every good story is improved by illustrations.

Whether your child has a future as an artist or is just occupying himself for the moment, he can have a good time for now, possibly impress his friends the next time they visit, and possibly develop more of an interest in reading, now that he's added a new layer of relating to literature.

Homemade Stationery

Materials: White paper, black crayon, photocopier, black pen or, if possible, typewriter

Here's another activity that works best when there's a photocopier in the house, as there are in more and more homes these days.

On a sheet of 8½-by-11-inch unlined white paper with no holes punched in it, the child writes in pen—or, if possible, types—her name and address. On the top or bottom of the sheet, she adds whatever design she wants in black crayon. Girls may want flowers, pictures of puppies or kittens, unicorns, curlicues, or fancy borders. Boys may prefer just a simple border around their names and addresses, or some more masculine picture such as fish, fishing poles, footballs, some other sports motif, a dinosaur, or a growling, fierce, ferocious lion. Either sex may like an abstract pattern—zigzags, swirls, or whatever else strikes their fancy.

If there's no photocopier, the child can prepare a sheet of personalized stationery for herself every time she's going to write a letter, using colored crayons to decorate the stationery instead of black. But if you have a photocopier in the house, or the child is planning a visit to Dad's or Mom's office and there's a copier there that she can use, all she needs to make up is one sheet of paper, copying from that. (The reason for using black pen and black crayon is that black reproduces the most sharply and darkly. If you don't have any black pens in the house, red copies better than blue.)

Of course, if your child is relying on an office copier, and it happens to copy in colors, she can make up the original of the stationery in colors, but as color copiers are still on the scarce side, and most copiers are black-and-white, the instructions above assume black-and-white copies and proceed accordingly.

Occupied by Design

Materials: Paper (graph paper works especially well here but isn't essential) and pencil with eraser

Everybody daydreams—adult or child, male or female. And often those daydreams take the form of imagining new and improved living quarters. A daydream may picture the ideal house to live in, one that's fantastically unreal, or the ideal way to rearrange one's room, something eminently practical.

Whether your child's dreams lead him in a direction that's purely a flight of fancy or work on a more practical plane, there's no reason he can't put pencil to paper and see what his dream looks like—if only on paper.

And he doesn't have to be limited to rooms and houses. How about designing a new school, or inventing a new toy or a radically new mode of transportation? (Again, we are talking about two different types of designs here—those which are practical and doable, and those which are in the realm of the wild blue yonder. Both are fun to think about and sketch out, regardless of whether the plan ever goes beyond paper.)

For the rearrangement of your child's room, he may wish to draw the room to scale, cut out scale representations of his furniture, and approach the whole thing very scientifically, or he may prefer the by-guess-and-by-gosh method, drawing in his bed, bookcase, dresser, toy chest, and so on in the spaces where he'd like to have them, then measuring afterward to see if it all fits where he's placed the various items, then erasing if it doesn't work.

He may even come up with a workable solution to a problem: shelves on one wall for storing games or books or toy animals, hooks on the wall for pjs and a robe, some kind of shoe stand for all those shoes that now lie messily all over. If he does come up with a practical and affordable suggestion, it's worth listening to; it might make the difference between a clean room and a messy one.

And if you do build or buy shelves or some other storage arrangement, and the room remains messy, he's just plain out of excuses. You can even make a "contract" with your child that you'll buy or build the extra bookcase, wall unit, or whatever if he'll clean the room weekly without a hassle, or keep it neat faithfully, or whatever seems to be fair for his part of the bargain.

But these projects needn't be purely practical. It's fun to let your imagination roam...even to roam far, far afield. And most kids love to imagine even more than adults do. Maybe your child would prefer to design the home he'd love to live in. It might have a glass roof so that he always feels he's camping out and he has the moon and stars for a ceiling at night. It might have one whole glass wall—perhaps on the east or west side so that he'll never miss a sunrise or sunset.

Perhaps his room would be a self-cleaning room, complete with some gadget to take care of that chore. Or maybe he'd like a room with a conveyor belt from the kitchen, for those times when you let your child eat in his room. How about a laundry chute from every bedroom to the laundry room, for quick and efficient disposal of dirty laundry? A TV in the ceiling over the bed, for watching while in bed at night? Special indoor-growing grass for the floor of his room, instead of a carpet? (So what if no such thing yet exists—I did say these designs didn't have to all be practical or feasible, didn't I?)

A budding ballerina might like one whole wall of her room to be mirrored, with a ballet barre. A young herpetologist might like built-in cages all along one wall for his or her pet snake collection—real or wished for.

How about a large empty room in the house with a floor suitable for roller-skating on? Or an ice rink attached to the house, suitable for ice-skating and hockey games? Or a bowling alley in the basement?

Now that his room is—perhaps practicably, perhaps not—rearranged and organized on paper, and he's designed a whole new house you'll never really live in, it's time to tackle designing a "fun" school. Or a practical one.

Now what about inventing a new toy? How about an invention that the whole world is waiting for, something to make life easier (or more fun) for adults or kids? What else can your child come up with?

57

Home Decorating

Materials: Magazines, paper, pen or pencil, scissors

This activity is fun for kids while at the same time teaching them a little about the costs of things in the real world out there. Has your son or daughter ever bugged you incessantly for a new dresser, a new bunk bed, a TV for her room, or some other unmanageable expense? Maybe it's that she thinks you're "made of money"—the old refrain of parents since time immemorial. But it's just as likely that she's simply unaware of what things cost.

Whether you choose to make your child aware of what your earnings are is your business, and the subject of a different activity in any case. But you can make her aware of the cost of various attractive items whether or not she has a firm grasp, a weak grasp, or none of how much money you have to work with in the first place.

Most kids have no concept of the dollar value of items they covet, whether the items are video games, new clothing, or a new house. This blissful ignorance of real-world costs also accounts in part for kids' cavalier treatment of household furnishings. So what if they get muddy footprints on the sofa? Wash it off. Buy a new sofa.

What? It's not washable? A new sofa costs a lot of money? How much *is* a lot of money, anyhow?

58

This activity will give your child a clue—while she has fun. It's simple…just offer the child a profusion of magazines (or newspapers—especially color ad supplements for furniture stores) with ads for various pieces of furniture for different rooms of the house. Include ads for such items as carpets, drapes, lamps, chandeliers, knickknacks and bric-a-brac, and even paintings to hang on the walls, if you wish.

Now tell your child to have fun browsing through the magazines and ads, selecting a sofa from here, end tables from there, a coffee table, a desk…whatever furniture she thinks would make an attractive living room. And to do the same for a master bedroom, a bedroom for herself, a kitchen, a dining room, and any other rooms you have in your house. Got a den? A guest room? One or more bedrooms for other kids in the family? They all need furnishing.

If your child never learns a thing about dollar values, she'll have fun furnishing a pretend house, or refurnishing your existing house. (If she prefers, she can pretend she's the grown-up, the master bedroom is hers, and the remaining bedrooms are her children's.)

She'll have fun picking and choosing, indulging her fantasies of a canopied bed, a home entertainment center with built-in audio components and a giant-screen TV, or a computer and computer desk of her very own for her room.

But she should keep track of the prices of all these furnishings, making note of them on a piece of paper as she clips out the pictures of the coveted items.

It's not very practical to paste down the items in place on a sheet of paper representing each room. The pictures won't be in scale to each other, and the computer might dwarf the bed, or a set of huge exercise equipment might look small enough to fit on a bookcase. But she can keep all the items for each room together. (Remind her to include such items as sheets for the bed, and a bedspread as well—there's more to a finished room than just furniture.)

When she's furnished a whole house—or just her own room, if she wants to undertake a less ambitious and less time-consuming project—ask her to tally up the cost of all the items she's selected. She's in for a shock.

Did she have the remotest clue it was so costly to furnish even one room? Did she know, during the past year of begging you and bugging you for a waterbed ("Please, Mom, please, huh, won't you, please, I really want it. Dale has one. Why can't I? C'mon, Mom, puh-*leeeeze?*") that they cost that much? Did she have even the slightest clue that the new dresser she wants costs more than the couple of dollars she may have imagined? Does she realize now, at least, that there's a hefty dollar value on all these things she covets, as well as on all the furniture she's been so rough on over the years with no thought to replacement cost?

For the child too young to appreciate monetary values, this home-decorating activity can still be fun minus the lesson in finances. Let her just cut out pretty pictures, furnishing a room or a whole house in furniture, carpets, drapes, and all that goes with it, in styles that appeal to her.

This can still lead, if you want it to, to a lesson in what goes together with what, in terms of style and appearance, even if you skip the high-finance aspect of the activity. Or don't use the activity to teach anything at all; just let the child have fun pretend-furnishing a house and let it go at that.

60

Reverse Silhouette Art
Materials: White and black construction paper, paste or glue, scissors

A striking picture can be created by pasting white cutouts on black construction paper. To accomplish this, draw the outline of your pictures—perhaps a sun, a couple of flowers, a tree, some clouds, or whatever tickles your fancy—on a sheet of white construction paper. Now cut the pictures out, and paste them (with the drawn-on side down, so any pencil lines don't show) on the black paper. Voila! Reverse silhouette art.

Personal Best

Basketball, of course, is a team game, a competitive game, a game in which one side tries to outscore the other. Even when two people play some form of basketball together, whether it's Horse or some other hoops game, they compete to see which will outscore the other.

Yet there's no question but that kids through the ages—and a fair number of adults as well—can be found practicing making baskets at the hoop on the garage on any pleasant afternoon or daylit evening, in or even out of basketball season.

Simply scoring is fun, even if there's no competition. Everyone likes to succeed, and scoring is success. There's a large measure of satisfaction to be derived from the chunk of the ball hitting the hoop and the swish as it goes through the net.

For some players, the chief consideration is that it's practice, practice, pratice that will make them better by the time they next compete against someone. For others, it's enough just to try shooting baskets, feeling a surge of satisfaction with each successful shot. And still others keep track of their scores from one hoops-shooting session to the next, always striving to improve their personal best.

That's what the games in this section are all about. They're all games that can be played competitively but that convey a certain satisfaction to their practitioners even when played solo. Each session can be fun as an experience unto itself. Score and enjoy it. Or the devotee of Flying Shuffleboard or Goofy Golf or any of the other games in here can keep track of her score from one session to the next, competing with herself, striving to always better her score.

Either way, of course, she has the satisfaction of knowing that, with so many practice sessions under her belt, she'll be that much sharper the next time there is someone to play with and she plays in competition.

Basket Bounce

Materials: One tennis ball or rubber ball, one coffee can

The rules for this one are easy enough; it's the game itself that isn't so easy. The idea is to make a "basket" by sinking the ball into the coffee can. The catch is that the ball must bounce at least once before entering the can.

The player may stand as close to the can he wants, but he must bounce the ball at least once, and the ball must remain in the can. If it bounces out again, there's no score. If it goes directly into the can without bouncing first, again there's no score. And if it knocks the can over, there's no score either. If the ball bounces more than once before entering the can, though, that's perfectly okay.

The player makes twenty attempts to bounce the ball into the can, scoring one point each time the ball bounces into the can and stays there. The total number of points garnered in the twenty attempts is his score.

Hints: Don't bounce the ball too hard. Don't bounce it right next to the can; start from a little distance away and you have a better chance at scoring.

Boxbaskets

Materials: Three or more shoeboxes or similar small boxes of similar depth, and several small objects such as jacks, erasers, checkers, individual thin rolled-up socks, or virtually anything else small and lightweight enough that a misthrow won't harm whatever the object flies against. It's best if you have at least five of these objects, and more is even better.

Boxbaskets is a tossing game. Aiming the small objects at the boxes from a distance of six to ten feet (depending on age), the player tries to score a "basket." Balls aren't good for this game; they tend to bounce out of the basket. The objects listed above work better.

64

The player lines the shoeboxes up in a straight line so that if the nearest box is six feet from the lag line, the line behind which she's standing as she tosses, the other boxes are progressively farther away. She assigns a point value to each box—the nearest box might be 5 points, the next one 10, and so on. Standing at the lag line, the player throws underhand.

The lag line doesn't have to be physically drawn; it can be a doorway, a certain floorboard, an imaginary line extending from the leg of the coffee table, the foot of the bed, the door to the bathroom, etc. For outdoor play, the lag line can be a crack in the sidewalk, an imaginary line extending from a certain tree, or any other landmark that lends itself to such use.

The player tosses all five (or ten, or whatever) of the small items at the boxes, adding up her score after they've all been tossed.

Basketbubbles

Materials: Bubble wand and bubble-blowing liquid, wastebasket or small box

This game combines the fun of blowing bubbles with a game in which one scores points. The player places a wastebasket or small box about six feet away from himself, then dips a bubble wand in bubble liquid and blows a bubble.

He must now direct the bubble into the basket by blowing on it...not too hard or he risks bursting the bubble. When he has the bubble located above the basket, he blows downward to direct it into the basket.

If the bubble lands on any other surface or bursts before setting into the basket, the player doesn't score. But if he guides the bubble successfully into the basket, he scores a point. He blows a total of twenty bubbles per game, trying to direct them with puffs of breath into the basket, and scoring one point for each successfully landed bubble.

65

TP Bowling

Materials: One rubber ball or tennis ball, ten cardboard tubes from toilet paper

Save your toilet paper cardboard, folks—there really is a use for it besides as a pretend spyglass for junior pirates. Here we see the tubes reincarnated as bowling pins.

Set ten tubes up in the same configuration as real bowling pins. Place them so that there is only a small bit of space between them.

Unlike real bowling, TP bowling allows the bowler only one ball to knock down all ten "pins" (but, hey, it's easier than real bowling!). You need a hallway, a driveway, or some other long area to play this in, as the bowler places herself behind a lag line about ten feet from the "pins" to roll the ball. The ball must be rolled; it may not be thrown, bounced, or skipped at the pins.

In consideration of the age of the players, scoring has been simplified. Score one point for each pin that's knocked down, and a 10-point bonus for a strike (all ten pins knocked down with one ball). A strike, in other words, nets a player 20 points. Anything else nets the player the number of knocked-down pins—1, 6, 9, or whatever. As each frame consists of only one ball, there are no spares in TP Bowling.

Checker Chase
Materials: Shoebox, ten checkers

This one requires a flat, hard playing surface—a table, a wood or flat linoleum or tile floor, not carpet, grass, a bed, or tile or linoleum with texture. In the middle of one end of a lidless shoebox, cut an opening that's an inch wide and slightly taller than a checker that's standing on its edge. Cut it at what would normally be the top of the box. In the middle of the other end, cut an opening equally tall and about two inches wide. Again, cut it at what would normally be the top of the box.

The player places the shoebox in what would normally be an upside-down position, so the holes at both ends are now touching the playing surface. The end with the smaller hole faces the player. If playing on a table, she should place the box about a foot from the edge. If playing on a hard floor, she simply positions herself about a foot away from the box.

Now the player rolls a checker toward the smaller opening. If the checker rolls through the opening and into the box, she scores 5 points. If it rolls out again at the other end, she scores an additional ten points. Repeat the process with all ten checkers, scoring the same way. Total score for the ten checkers is the player's score for the round.

As with the other games in this section, this game can be played competitively but is also good for solo fun, with the player trying to improve her previous high score.

Flying Shuffleboard

Materials: String and scissors, or chalk; cardboard; optional: paint or crayons

Shuffleboard has long been associated with shipboard games and retirement community fun. But this version, involving tossing cardboard rather than pushing wood, is well suited to the younger set.

If playing indoors, the player delineates his target with string as follows: He cuts a length of string about two feet long and lays it down in a circle. Now he cuts two more lengths of string each longer than the previous, perhaps four feet and six feet long respectively, and lays them in concentric circles around the first string. He now has something resembling a bull's-eye.

If playing outdoors on grass, he can delineate his target the same way. If playing on pavement, he can simply draw chalk circles instead.

He'll be aiming cardboard projectiles at these targets. He should cut the projectiles from cardboard in any shapes he wants. The width at the widest point of each projectile should roughly equal at least half the width of the inner circle of the target. If he wishes, he can decorate the projectiles with crayon or paint, though this is strictly optional.

With either chalk or another length of string, he should mark a lag line at a point about ten feet from the target. (If he finds it's either too easy or impossible to score from that distance, he can adjust it.)

The inner circle of the target will be worth the most points—say 10. The middle circle will be worth less—say 5 points. And the outer circle will be worth the least—say 1 point. (Any other scoring system is fine too—100, 50, and 25, or 5, 3, and 1—as long as the middle circle carries the highest value, and the others progressively lower.)

The game of Flying Shuffleboard is very forgiving. It's not necessary to score a projectile entirely within the inner circle to score the highest point value. Merely getting some part of a projectile inside the inner circle qualifies the player for the highest score. Similarly, if a projectile lands straddling the outer and middle circles, the player scores for hitting the middle circle, and if the projectile is partly outside the target and partly in the outer circle, the player scores for that circle.

The more projectiles your child cuts out of cardboard, the more he'll be able to throw per round. Say he throws three projectiles and is using a 10-5-1 scoring system. The first projectile misses the target altogether, the second touches the middle circle, and the third touches the inner circle. His score for the round is 15 (0 + 10 + 5).

As he continues playing, he'll try to improve his score from one game to the next. If he finds he's getting too good at it, he should move the lag line farther back to make the game harder.

Slingshot Buckets

Materials: Slingshot (can be homemade), projectiles (such as rocks, beans, marbles), receptacle to aim at (such as coffee can, wastebasket)

Remember those commercials that advocated, with tongue in cheek, crossing two divergent sports and coming up with a bizarre combination like sumo high-diving? Suppose you crossed slingshot shooting with basketball? You'd have Slingshot Buckets! Players can use a slingshot purchased ready-made at the store, or fashion their own out of a bent coat hanger or forked twig with a rubber band stretched over it.

Either way, it needs to be used sensibly and respectfully; carelessly used slingshots have hurt people. Your child should play outdoors or in some other area, such as a basement, where no people, pets, or furniture are in harm's way.

The player sets up the target—a wastebasket or coffee can is good—angled so that it's tilted slightly toward her if possible, and takes a few practice shots to see how far away she should stand. Too close and it's too easy, no fun. Too far away and it's too difficult, too frustrating, also no fun. I can't recommend a specific number of feet; suitable distance will depend on the size of the target, player's age and skill, and how sophisticated the slingshot is.

If the player sets up only one target, she scores a point each time she lands a projectile in it. She can also set up several coffee cans, wastebaskets, etc., crediting herself 1 point for scoring into the nearest or largest, 3 points for an intermediate-sized or -distanced one, and 5 points for the hardest one to score into.

After shooting ten projectiles, player adds up her score. Now she shoots another ten, seeing if she can better that score. She continues shooting ten at a time for as long as she wants, always trying to improve her previous best score.

Take Me in to the Ball Game

Materials: Varied, for different games, including one or more of the following: rubber ball, wadded paper, empty wastebasket, blocks, length of string, Popsicle stick, rolled-up sock, rolled-up newspaper

Indoor ball games can be fun *and* improve a child's aim and accuracy. And, just the way kids can practice solo at a basketball hoop for hours, they can have fun solo with indoor ball games, whether they're keeping score or not.

A good scorekeeping plan is to see how many shots out of ten your child can make. He then takes another ten shots and sees if he can improve his average.

Now, what kind of ball games are we talking about?

Most of them are basketball-type games. Shooting an object into a basket puts lamps and other objects in less jeopardy than batting an object around. Your child's basket will probably be an empty wastebasket, though there are certainly other objects such as empty boxes of an appropriate size that can be used instead.

One projectile that can be safely aimed at an impromptu basket is a wadded-up piece of paper. To make the task more difficult, the wastebasket can be set up on a piece of furniture, such as a desk or dresser in the child's room.

Or your child can simply shoot at a wastebasket on the floor, from a distance that makes it tougher to make the shot. This provides an easier target than a wastebasket elevated on furniture, which depending on his skill level may be a good thing. Too, if the target is on the floor, not up on furniture, it's easier for a small child to retrieve the paper after scoring.

Wadded-up paper can also be used for a batting game, if your child tosses the paper up in the air, then swats at it with his open hand. The challenge here can be to swat the paper a certain distance—say, as far as the bed, or beyond the bookcase—or to get it to land in a certain place—say, within a circle of blocks, or a target created by cutting a length of string and laying it down on the floor in a circle.

Another object that can be aimed at a wastebasket or other container with relatively little hazard (but more than a wadded-up piece of paper) is a marble.

A marble can also be used in the manner of a bowling ball, aiming it between two blocks that have been set perhaps three inches apart on the floor (more or less, depending on your child's age and skillfulness). If your child finds he is scoring consistently, he can either decrease the space between the blocks or increase the distance across which he is rolling the marble. Conversely, if he's hardly scoring at all, he needs to move the blocks farther apart or move his starting point nearer the goal.

If, instead of rolling the marble, he hits it between the blocks with a Popsicle stick, he's now got a golf game going.

If you have an unfinished basement with nothing breakable in it, your child can play ball games with a rubber ball, perhaps setting a wastebasket on top of the washer or dryer, if those are down in the basement, and aiming the rubber ball into the basket.

The basement is a good place, too, to take that wadded-up paper and practice kicking it over a makeshift goalpost, such as a piece of string tied across a short distance, perhaps tied to the backs of two chairs or whatever's handy in the basement.

Yet another projectile suitable for both basketball and bare-handed swatting is a rolled-up sock.

Of course if you have a backyard, where the child can play these games without fear of knocking over lamps, and if the weather's nice enough for playing outdoors, standard sports equipment can be used. Or a rolled-up newspaper can be used as a bat that will carry a sock or wadded-up paper farther, but not as far or dangerously as a real bat will carry a real ball.

That same rolled-up newspaper can be used to knock a rolled-up sock between two blocks for another version of indoor golf.

There are probably even more possibilities for safe indoor ball games. Empty tubes from paper towels make bats or golf clubs. Wadded-up aluminum foil can be a ball of various sizes depending how much you use. Just look around and use your imagination.

Sheet Ball

Materials: One sheet that was destined for the rag pile (or use a blanket, bedspread, large drape, or similar item that you don't mind having cut up), scissors, clothesline or rope, ball (probably a tennis ball or rubber ball); optional: clothespins, paint

Sheet Ball is another game that's fun to play alone as a solo self-challenge as well as in competition with others. For this game, your child (or you) needs to cut various holes in a sheet. Some should be just a little larger than the ball she intends to throw (most probably a tennis ball or rubber ball), while others should be much larger.

Assign a point value to each hole, with the smaller holes being worth more than the larger ones. If desired, your child can paint the point value below or above each hole. It doesn't matter if the large holes are 1 point, the medium holes 3 points, and the small holes 5 points, or if the system is 5-10-15, or 25-50-100, just so some sort of similar ratio is maintained. How many holes she cuts is optional—one of each size, two of each size, or more.

String up a rope or clothesline and suspend the sheet from it. Pick a spot that offers two trees, a tree and a fencepost, or some other suitable uprights to tie the rope to. Also, the spot should have nothing vulnerable behind it, such as windows. You don't want the child to score 10 points and break a window at the same time!

You can either hang the sheet with clothespins or fold just enough over the top to balance the sheet and keep it on the line, without it draping down so far that it overlaps and blocks any holes.

73

Decide on a suitable spot for your child to stand, not so near that scoring is ridiculously easy, nor so far away that it's impossible. If she has more than one ball to throw, she won't have to retrieve it after every throw, but in any case she gets five throws per round, and she adds up her score from the five throws to get her score for the round.

Can she beat that score next round?

Indoor Mini-Golf
Materials: Ruler, rubber ball or tennis ball or jacks ball (best choice of the three if you have one), coffee cans or similar-sized cans, paper and pen or pencil for scoring

You may want to keep this game out of the living room if you have expensive china knickknacks or precariously perched, fragile lamps. On the other hand, if you have a kidproofed living room, a family room, and a couple of hallways, they along with your child's room can all be part of your indoor mini-golf course.

The number of holes on your mini-golf course doesn't have to be nine or eighteen, as in real golf. It can be three, fifteen, or any other number, according to how many coffee cans you have available and how much room there is to set up the course in areas where a stray ball isn't likely to wreak havoc.

Your child needs to establish the location of the holes (coffee cans laid on their sides) and the tees (purely imaginary—just pick a spot on which to lay the ball down for teeing off). More than one hole in a room is perfectly permissible. Setting up hazards is fine but not necessary. Enough hazards probably exist naturally (such as a sofa or bed for the ball to roll underneath). A two-stroke penalty can be assessed at any hazard; should the ball roll into the open closet, out the open front door, down the stairs, or into the dog's water dish, remove it, set it at the nearest playable spot, and take a two-stroke penalty.

It's also possible to play this game outdoors. (See also Goofy Golf and Nickel Golf, which follow). But if playing indoors, your duffer needs to be careful when swinging the ruler "golf club" not to swing wildly and knock anything over or strike the ball in such a way as to make it bounce or loft.

Just as golfers can play alone when the links are empty, your young mini-golfer can play alone too. Golf is a great sport for playing to improve one's own score, without competition with another player being essential.

Goofy Golf

Materials: Newspaper golf club (for which you need several sections of newspaper and some tape), sock ball (for which you need several of those mismatched socks you have lying around), blocks or other similar objects to delineate goals

The player should first create his golf club, by rolling several sections of newspaper together and taping the roll closed. Whether he'll need two sections or five depends on whether your newspaper's sections are thick or thin. He'll need something sturdy enough to knock around a sock ball without collapsing.

The sock ball is simply a few socks rolled together. Again, he may need two socks or five, depending on whether they're a small child's thin cotton summer socks, Dad's big, thick, winter-weight socks, or some combination.

The "holes" in Goofy Golf aren't literally holes; rather, he'll be aiming the ball between two delineating markers, such as blocks, that have been set close together. How close? The area between them should be wider than the sock ball by about half again the width of the sock ball.

If your child hits the sock ball between the blocks (or other markers) he's sunk the putt. If he hits the ball beyond the blocks but not between them, he needs to hit it back again and try again. Only by hitting the ball between the two markers and going in the right direction can he claim he's sunk the putt.

This game can be played either indoors or out. Either way, your young duffer is likely to encounter hazards. If he's playing outdoors, the ball might roll into the flower bed and nestle in the pansies; if he's playing indoors, the ball might roll under the bed. Either way, if the ball is unplayable after rolling into a hazard, the player needs to retrieve it, drop it at the nearest playable spot, and take a two-stroke penalty (add two strokes to his score for that hole).

76

Again, as with the Mini-Golf game above, golf is a great game for playing alone and doesn't require a competitive player to play with.

Fore!

Nickel Golf
Materials: One coin; optional: string

This golf game, unlike the two above, does require digging holes—or at least one hole—in the lawn. But the holes are minimal—teacup size, actually, or perhaps even a tad shallower than that. Dig the heel of a shoe into the turf and turn in a circle. You now have a hole. You can try to sink your nickel (penny, quarter, dime) into that one hole over and over, or you can make several other holes if you wish, though really one hole is sufficient.

Start from a lag line as far back from the hole as you can place it without it being in your neighbor's yard—at least fifteen feet, though farther is even better. The lag line can be delineated by digging a line with your heel, or you can place a length of string to create your starting point.

Throw the coin at the hole. That's one "stroke." Keep an eye on the coin as it flies through the air. Now follow its path and pick it up where it landed, throwing it at the hole again. Keep throwing till it lands in the cup and stays there. The number of throws it took to get it in the hole is your score for that hole.

Return to the lag line to begin the second hole and every hole thereafter. The game can be a traditional nine or eighteen holes, or any other number you want. As in the two games above, if the coin lands someplace from which it's unplayable, retrieve it, stand in the nearest playable spot, and throw it from there, taking a two-stroke penalty for the hazard.

Variations:

• Roll the coin to the hole instead of throwing it. (This won't work if your ground is terribly uneven or your grass needs cutting.)

• "Tee off" by standing with your back to the hole and throwing the coin over your shoulder without looking. Subsequent throws are in the usual manner.

• Tee off by throwing the coin down onto the ground so that it skips. It must skip, or bounce, at least once or the stroke doesn't count and must be taken over. Subsequent throws are in the usual manner.

• Tee off by flipping the coin off the end of the index or middle finger, using the thumb. The coin should spin in the air as it is propelled toward (hopefully!) the hole. Subsequent throws are in the usual manner.

• All strokes are taken by flipping the coin off the end of the index or middle finger, as above. This will make the game much harder, but for the child who finds the basic version too easy, this version will offer a much greater challenge.

Unlike the two golf games above, this is strictly for outdoor play. But like the other two games, it is perfectly suited for solo play.

Solitaires & Similar Solos

Here is a small sampling of solitaire games of various sorts. Some are played with cards, some with dominoes, and some with other equipment. Some, like Ace-Deuce-Three, are quiet pastimes; others, like Button Baseball, are a little more physical; and Dribbler's Squares is a fully active game. But regardless of other classifications, all the games are designed to be enjoyed by one player, and all are fun.

Skip Two

Materials: Ordinary deck of cards (bridge/poker, not pinochle)

Whoever named this game couldn't count. Despite the name, you actually skip one pile of cards in seeking a suitable place to play each card you turn over. But I'm getting ahead of myself. Here are the rules:

Shuffle a deck of ordinary (poker/bridge) cards and place them face down on the table. Turn the top card face-up and lay it down. This is the foundation of your home pile.

Turn up the next card. If it matches the card in the home pile, either in *suit* or in *number,* place it on the home pile. Otherwise start a new pile to the right of the home pile. Now turn over a third card.

If your second card matched the first, and you only have one pile of cards, follow the above instructions for the third card: If it matches, place it on the home pile, and if it doesn't, place it to the right.

If your second card didn't match the first, and you have two piles of cards, you can discard onto the rightmost pile but not the one to its immediate left. Once you have established a third pile, however, you get into the "skip two" (actually skip one) aspect—you are permitted to play onto the rightmost pile *or skip one and play onto the pile two over from the rightmost pile.*

Now that you have three (or more) piles, this will continue to be your procedure. As you turn over each card, you may play it on the rightmost pile or skip one and lay the card on the pile two over from the rightmost pile. Any time you cannot make either of these two moves, you must start a new pile, which must be to the right of the rightmost pile.

At some point, a card you play on one of the piles may make it match the top card on the pile to its left or two over from it. Example: Your top cards are a 7 of spades, Jack of diamonds, Queen of clubs, and 2 of hearts. You play a 2 of diamonds on the 2 of hearts, and now it matches, in suit, the Jack of diamonds two piles over. You can now move that whole pile topped by the 2 of diamonds onto the pile topped by the Jack of diamonds.

In some cases this may have a domino effect on other piles. If the 2 of diamonds lands next to, or two to the right of, another pile topped by a 2 or a diamond, you can now move the whole pile topped by the 2 of diamonds onto the other pile topped by the 2 or the diamond, next to it or two to the left. Continue consolidating your piles in this fashion until you're out of possible moves.

Continue turning over all the cards in the deck, following these rules. The aim of the game is to wind up with the fewest possible piles when you've turned over all the cards, with one pile being a perfect game.

Ace-Deuce-Three
Materials: Deck of cards (bridge/poker, not pinochle)

The rules of this game are simple enough, but winning it isn't nearly so easy. Shuffle a standard fifty-two-card deck and keep the deck face-down. Now turn the first card over and say "Ace." If it's anything but an ace, keep going, turning the next card over and saying "Deuce." Again, if it's anything but a deuce, keep going, saying "Three" (or "Trey" if you prefer to call them that), and hoping, again, that it's not a three you turn over. Continue in this manner all the way through "King," starting over again with "Ace" after that.

If at any point you turn over the card you had called, the game's over. You've lost. If you can get through all fifty-two cards, called "Ace" through "King" in four sequences, without once turning over the card you called, you've won.

Easy rules to remember. Hard game to win.

Domino Knockdown
Materials: Dominoes, marble, flat surface

A flat playing surface is needed for this one—a wood, linoleum, or flat tile floor, or conceivably a low-pile carpet, or else a large tabletop, large board, or something similarly flat. The child can start with ten dominoes, setting them upright on the short end so that they're standing tall. She should place them approximately three-fourths of an inch apart from each other, in a straight line, not side by side but with the front of one domino facing the back of the next.

83

Now she rolls a marble from a distance of about one foot from the lead domino. Can she knock down all ten dominoes with one roll?

If, trying it repeatedly, she finds it too much of a challenge (due to her age or dexterity), she should do one of three things: set the dominoes closer together, use fewer dominoes, or roll the marble from a smaller distance. If, on the other hand, she finds she's knocking down all ten consistently, she can increase the challenge by taking the opposite steps: set the dominoes farther apart, use more dominoes, or roll the marble from a greater distance.

Additionally, if she gets very good at this and seeks a greater challenge, she can try setting the dominoes up in a staggered pattern, with the second domino slightly to the left of the first, the third slightly to the right again (directly in line with the first), the fourth to the left (directly in line with the second), and so on. Can she knock them all down now? What if she arranges them in a curve…can she still knock them down with one roll of the marble?

She can also try other arrangements, and even experiment with other domino tricks, after she masters the basic Knockdown game.

Happy bowling!

Idiot's Delight
(Domino Survivors)
Materials: A box of dominoes (incomplete box is fine)

You don't need a full box of dominoes to play Idiot's Delight. If you're missing the 3-2 or 6-blank (or even more than one tile), you can still play Idiot's Delight with the remainder.

It's essentially a mindless game (hence the name), and yet for a child who's into statistics, it can become a source of great record-keeping involvement.

Idiot's Delight should be played on a soft surface—a carpet, a bed, or even the grass outdoors. The child tosses all the dominoes *gently and lightly* into the air. Those that fall face-up are "survivors." Removing all the ones that fell face-down, he tosses the "survivors" up into the air again, again removing those that fell face-down. He keeps going till only one face-up domino remains. That one is the winner.

For the child who's not statistically oriented, this mindless pursuit is essentially it...seeing how many tosses it takes to come up with a winner, and what the winner is. A pleasant pastime with which to occupy a brief period. Ah, but for the child who's a statistics nut, there's a veritable treasure trove of data to be kept here.

How many rounds will result in no winners—the dominoes are tossed, and tossed, and tossed, and on the last toss, they *all* land face-down? How many times will each tile win, and is there one tile that repeats frequently? How many tosses will it take to get a winner in the average game? What's the fewest tosses that result in a winner? What's the largest number of times he can toss them and still have tiles left in the game?

As simple fun, this game can be a good time-killer for the child who has ten minutes till dinner or Scouts or some other activity and doesn't quite know how to fill that time. As a matter of statistical interest for the child who's statistically oriented, it can be an absorbing activity consuming hours of time.

Solo Concentration

Materials: Deck of cards (bridge/poker, not pinochle), paper and pen or pencil

Whether you remember this game from the TV version or as the popular kids' game it was even before the TV incarnation, the premise is probably familiar to you: Players turn over a card, try to match it by turning over a second card, and get to keep both cards if they're a match.

A solo version of Concentration can be played by one player, playing not against one or more other players but against her own previous score. For instance, if it took twenty minutes to get all the pairs last time, can she get them all in nineteen or less this time? Here's how to proceed:

Start by laying out all fifty-two cards (or fifty-four with two jokers) in rows. You're not going to have even rows. Don't worry about it. You might have ten rows of five cards each, with two extra cards (four if playing with jokers) in one row. Or you might have some other configuration. There is no one right way.

Now the player turns over one card—any card she wants. She next turns over a second card. If they match in number (two 7s, two Jacks, etc.), she has a pair. She removes them and places them to the side. If they don't match, she turns them both face-down again, trying to remember what each card was and where it was located. If she has not paired two cards, she makes a mark on the paper, indicating one round. If she did pair, the round is not over yet, and no mark should be made.

Now she turns another card over. If she didn't pair on the first round, and this card is a match to one of the cards she turned over on the first round, she tries to remember where that card was and turn it over. If she succeeds, and now has a match, she removes that pair. If not, she turns both cards face-down again. Again, if she hasn't paired, she makes a mark on the paper.

She continues in this manner. A round is over whenever the player doesn't succeed in pairing. She then makes a mark on the paper, indicating another round. When a player does pair, the round isn't over, and she keeps turning cards over, making a mark only when she fails to pair.

When all fifty-two (or fifty-four) cards have been matched up, the player counts the number of rounds it took her to pair up the whole board. That's her score for the game. Next game—whether it's immediately thereafter or a week later—she tries to do better.

Variations: To make the game easier, remove half the deck and play only with Ace–7 or 8–King, or only the red cards, or only the black cards.

To make the game harder, require that cards match not only in number but color. That is, a 9 of diamonds and a 9 of clubs would not be a match. Only red 9s or black 9s would match each other.

Heads or Tails—What Are the Odds?

87

Materials: One or more coins or sports cards

If you flip a coin, what are the odds it will come up heads? Is there any difference between a penny and a quarter in the number of times heads versus tails will come up? Does it make a difference if you toss it higher in the air? What if you flip it as you throw it upward?

How about a baseball card or football card? Does one of those more often come up heads than tails, or more often tails than heads? In ten flips, how many times will heads come up? How about if you flip it twenty times? Fifty? One hundred?

Besides coins and sports cards, what else does your child have that's suited to flipping heads-or-tails? How often will it come up one side versus the other? Is there anything your child can do to influence which side will come up?

Your budding scientist or mathematician may become surprisingly engrossed in the statistical complexities, even to keeping elaborate records of the number of times the experiment was performed and the results each time. But don't suggest to him that there's anything mathematical or scientific about the experiment. If it starts to sound suspiciously like a school-oriented problem, suddenly it will lose its appeal. Statistics? Science? Math? That's schoolwork—ugh! But playing with baseball cards or money? Now *that's* fun!

Dribbler's Squares
Materials: Basketball or playground ball, sidewalk marked off into squares

This game's rules are simple; successfully playing it is not so simple. The playing field is the sidewalk in front of your home. The game can be played on as few as four or five squares of sidewalk (if your child is so small that you feel you need to tell her to stay in front of the house while playing), or she can utilize the whole length of the sidewalk from one corner to the next.

As simple as the game is, it can keep a child occupied for a long time with its challenge. She'll play it once, get out on five, and start over to see if, with another attempt, she can make it up to six this time, or beat her all-time personal best.

The game consists of dribbling, or in other words bouncing, the ball a set number of times in each consecutive square of the sidewalk. The first time she traverses the playing field, she's to bounce the ball once in each square. When she reaches the end of the playing field (whether that's the corner, or the fifth square down, or the start of the Robinsons' driveway), she turns around and dribbles once in that square again, then once in the next square, once in the next, and so on till she arrives back at the Start square.

Now she dribbles the ball twice in each square, again making her way down the length of the sidewalk and back again. Then three times, four, and so on till she misses.

What's a miss? Not dribbling the right number of times in each square, holding or catching the ball (other than at the end of the playing field), or dribbling onto a crack, rather than cleanly in a square, or stepping off the sidewalk ("out of bounds"). It is *not* a miss for the child's foot to step on a crack.

Besides being fun and a challenge, the game builds skill in dribbling, a useful ability if the child is ever going to play basketball, even if only in gym class.

If you live in the country, or the rural suburbs, and you have no sidewalk, she can still play if she marks off sidewalk-sized squares on the driveway with a piece of chalk. Or, if you live on a quiet street that's safe to play in, she can chalk squares there.

Variation 1—Skipover: A more experienced dribbler can make the challenge a little tougher by dribbling the ball not in every square but in every other square. It requires more control of the ball to move it three feet along the sidewalk rather than ten inches forward.

Variation 2—Skipover and Back: In this variation, for even more experienced ball-handlers, the dribbler skips forward a square, then drops back to the one skipped, then repeats the pattern.

Example: The player is on Three. She dribbles three times in square 1, then skips square 2 and dribbles three times in square 3, then goes back to square 2 and dribbles three times there, skips square 3 and dribbles three times in square 4, goes back to square 3 and dribbles three times, skips square 4, and dribbles three times in square 5, and continues that way to the end of the playing field (if square 5 isn't the end). Reaching the end, she turns around and does the same thing in reverse to return.

Not only is this variation more challenging, it's more time-consuming as well.

Variation 3—Neverstop: In this variation, the player isn't allowed to catch or hold the ball at the end of each round; when she completes One, she pivots and starts right in on Two without a break, without holding the ball, without resting. A good skill-builder for budding basketball players, this variation will get kids used to thinking of dribbling as a fluid, uninterrupted activity.

Variation 4—Simplicity: This is for the youngest set, kids not yet quite ready to play even the basic version successfully. The child is called upon to bounce the ball a set number of times in each square, again without bouncing it on a crack or stepping off the sidewalk, but after bouncing the requisite number of times in each square, the child may catch the ball and carry it to the next square. She doesn't have to make the progress from square to square a part of the fluid motion of dribbling.

For a budding basketball player at the youngest age level, who can't even accomplish this variation, suggest she bounce the ball and catch it the requisite number of times in each square. This is a far cry from the true basic game of Dribbler's Squares, but your child can work her way up from this subvariation to the Simplicity variation to the true game as she gets more skillful with age and practice.

Button Baseball

Materials: Small box, carton, or box top; scissors; buttons, coins, washers, or similar; if the carton or box top isn't a solid, pale color, you also need plain paper to cover the carton or box top, and glue to hold it on

Though Button Baseball is a competitive game, it doesn't have to be played by two people. It can be played by one player making the moves for two imaginary teams. The competition, then, becomes one between the two imaginary teams, with the sole player keeping track of the outcome. Will the Mets beat the Yankees? (In Button Baseball, the two teams don't have to be in the same real-life league. They don't even have to be named after real-life teams; your two teams could be the Marvels and the Miracles, or the Powerhouse and the Pinnacle, or any names you want.)

Scoring is determined by maneuvering a button around the playing field (hence the name), and that playing field is drawn and cut on the top of a box, or simply a box top without the box. It should be at least 8 by 10 inches and probably no larger than 15 by 24 inches. Those cardboard containers that hold twelve or twenty-four cans of soda make good Button Baseball stadiums.

Since the player is going to draw on the box top, it needs to be a solid, light color. If it's dark or has writing on it, he should paste some light brown packaging paper, white typing paper, or other suitable paper to the lid.

Now he sketches a baseball diamond on the flat upper surface of the box top. There is no regulation distance between bases in Button Baseball, but the diamond should be in the normal shape of a baseball diamond, with the bases laid out accordingly. The actual size will depend on the size of box top he's using. Home plate should be near the bottom edge of the box top, with first and third bases near the edges of the playing field, and he'll want to leave room for an outfield behind second base, in the usual spot.

Next he needs to cut a circular hole at each of the four bases (home plate included). The exact size of the hole is optional, as a larger hole will make it easier to score, and a smaller hole will be tougher. Generally two to three inches in diameter is a good size range.

He needs to cut three more holes next, in approximately the positions that would be occupied by the left, center, and right fielders. He should also draw base paths between the bases, as well as a pitcher's mound, and a slender path between the mound and home plate. These paths are not essential to the play of the game but add a certain air of realism to the play, making the game more enjoyable.

The holes get labeled as follows: First base is Single, second base is Double, and third base is Triple. The holes at home plate, left field, and right field are Out. And the hole in center field is labelled Home Run.

To play, your child stands or kneels at a distance of five or six feet from the box top. (Standing may be okay if the box top is on a table or the player is quite short, but otherwise kneeling may be preferable.) The methodology here is to toss buttons (or coins or washers or anything similar in size and weightiness) at the holes in the box top. Obviously, he wants to aim for the Home Run hole if possible, and try to avoid Out. If he fails to score into any hole, the throw doesn't count.

There are no strikes or balls in the most basic version of Button Baseball. There are only hits and outs. When the player sinks his button in a hole, he advances (or is called out) according to the hole's label. After three outs, the side is retired.

He does not advance an actual marker around the base paths, however. Anything on the playing field might get in the way of an incoming button's movement, so the location of base runners along the base paths has to be kept track of mentally, or on a separate sheet of paper.

It is a matter of little importance which team is up first or has "last licks." There is no particular advantage either way. The solo player can determine the order of his imaginary teams' batting by tossing a coin and calling "Heads" or "Tails" for one team or the other, or by any other method he prefers.

93

Variations:

• All the holes on the field are marked as hits, the three outfield slots as singles, and home plate as a home run. In this case, a player whose button fails to drop through one of the holes is out.

• The field can be constructed with the various holes being cut different sizes. The hole for a home run should be the smallest, the holes for singles larger, and for an out treacherously large.

• An extra hole can be added, somewhere out of the field of play such as off to the lower right or left, marked Walk.

• Instead of tossing buttons or coins, the player can use tiddlywinks, propelling them in the standard tiddlywink manner.

Batter up!

Skill Builders

The activities in this section will all help your child build one useful skill or another, yet they're all activities he'll enjoy. The skills are diversified, but the outcome is the same—learning while having fun.

Knowledge Challenges

Materials: Paper and pen or pencil

Sometimes your child can be diverted from boredom by a challenge to her knowledge. But to keep it from seeming as if he's back in school and taking a pop quiz, you might want to offer a reward if she gets the answers right. Or you can even admit that this is an activity that's "good for her," not just fun, and point out that school isn't just for learning stuff that seeps out of the brain when the bell rings at three o'clock. Your child should know and remember much of what she's learned even after she's been tested on it at school and moved on to another chapter.

For instance...does she know all fifty states? Challenge her to write them down on a piece of paper. (That should keep her busy for a while!) If she succeeds, ask her to go back and write the appropriate capital next to each state. Depending on your child's age and grade level, you can ask questions as simple as "Name as many birds [trees, flowers, African animals] as you can think of," or as difficult as "Name all the elements and give the abbreviation for each." Other possible questions: "Name the oceans of the world," "Write as many geographic place-names beginning with 'A' as you can think of," "List all the languages you can name," and "List all the classical composers you can think of."

Rolling (in) Wealth

Materials: Jar of loose coins

If your household is like most, you've got a jar, a milk jug, a coffee can, or a vase full of loose change stashed somewhere. As the pennies, nickels, dimes and quarters mount, so do your visions of how all these coins will fatten your bank account.

But first the coins have to be rolled.

And that's where your child comes into the picture.

First the coins have to be separated by type—a good sorting exercise for your child. Differentiating quarters from pennies should be no problem for most kids, but pennies and dimes are awfully similar, and to a young enough child, even nickels and quarters can be confusing.

Then the coins have to be counted—a good counting exercise. Rather than count from one to fifty (in the case of pennies and dimes) or forty (nickels and quarters), and risk getting up to forty-eight and losing track, it's simpler if he counts by tens, stacking each group of ten and going on to the next.

Then four stacks of ten can be put together to make a roll of forty, or five stacks of ten can make a roll of fifty—a good lesson in multiplication.

The forty or fifty coins have to be eased into the roll—good practice in dexterity—and the roll has to be sealed.

If your bank is one that requires your name or account number on rolls, it's best if you write that information before you stuff the rolls. If your child writes well enough, he can help you with that phase of the operation too.

If you want to, you can reward the child for his help by giving him a roll of pennies to put in his own bank account, if he has a college fund. Or let him keep them in his piggy bank, if the college fund isn't meaningful enough to the child. But a reward isn't absolutely necessary; not every chore brings a reward, and the satisfaction of a job well done should reward him for his efforts.

There's one other, less tangible reward: The child who helps roll coins can see for himself that saving does pay off, that a lowly dime (or penny), and another and another and a couple of dozen more can add up to a roll of appreciable worth, and that a number of such rolls can really fatten a bank account.

And that's a lesson worth far more than just practice in sorting, counting, or multiplying, or an exercise in manual dexterity!

The King Was in His Countinghouse

Materials: Jar of loose coins

Before you next roll up the loose coins in your coffee can or mayonnaise jar (see Rolling [in] Wealth, above), you can use them to help your child get a little practice in handling and counting money, a necessary skill as she gets older.

I'm assuming, for this activity, that your child already knows the difference between the different denominations, and that you won't have to stand there with her, patiently explaining that this is a penny and this is a dime, even if she doesn't yet know by heart that ten pennies are equal to one dime.

There are different exercises (you can call them "games" to your child) that will help make her more comfortable with managing money. The first is to ask her to make one pile of each denomination of coins that equals a dollar. It may take her a while to count out one hundred pennies, but she'll get a good feel for the interrelationship of the denominations as she counts out one hundred pennies, twenty nickels, ten dimes, and four quarters. (She'll also be too busy for quite a while to complain that she's booooored!)

Another exercise is to ask your child to make up a pile of coins equal to $1.00, another equal to $1.20, and a third equal to $1.75, each pile to contain *at least one coin of each denomination*. (If you're not yet rolling in wealth in that jar, choose smaller target amounts for each pile, to be sure there's enough of each type of coin that your child can fulfill the request.)

Next offer your child this challenge: "How many different ways can you get a pile of coins to add up to one dollar?" Next: "Can you make a pile of six coins that total up to one dollar?" "How about seven coins?"

You can offer the child each challenge, then go off to do something on your own, returning when she's finished, or you can keep the child occupied in the same room you're in while you're balancing the checkbook, cooking, reading, working, or doing a crossword. Your attention will be required more than for most of the activities in this book, but it doesn't have to be constant or total.

This next exercise, though, will require your presence. Give the child a pile of mixed coins totalling one dollar. Now ask, "If you give me two dimes, a nickel, and a penny, how much money have you got left?" Ask other, similar questions, and get the child used to making change.

If she becomes properly proficient at understanding money as well as at making change, she'll never fall for the old playground ploy of "Got two dimes for a nickel?" nor will anyone ever shortchange *your* kid.

Just What Is a "Countinghouse"?

Materials: A house (an apartment is fine—anything with at least a few rooms)

"The king was in his countinghouse, counting out his money." That's what the nursery rhyme says, but what *is* a "countinghouse," anyhow? When I was a kid, I wondered. Didn't you? Your child probably has wondered too.

Your house can become a "countinghouse" in quite a different sense—a house in which your child practices counting, in this silly little game that will occupy a small part of a bored day and give him practice with numbers at the same time. Kids old enough to multiply may not fall for this, but any child old enough to count past one hundred and young enough to enjoy showing off his skill is a suitable target for the following suggestion:

"Go into the living room and count to one hundred. Then go into the kitchen and keep counting till you get to two hundred. Keep going, till you've counted one hundred in every room in the house. Then tell me how far you've got."

If your child can't count past 100, you can assign him to count up to ten in the living room, keep going to twenty in the kitchen, and so on, though it won't use up nearly as much time.

Shop 'Till You Drop

Materials: Magazine pictures of various attractive items, large collection of assorted coins

Here's yet another use for that jarful of coins that's been accumulating over the months. Before your child rolls them up (see Rolling [in] Wealth, page 98), she can use them to practice counting money and paying the correct amount, a skill every child needs to learn.

Prepare for this activity by cutting out magazine pictures of items that might look attractive to your child. Assign a price to each item—not a real price, but one that will require your child to come up with a combination of different coins. Write the price alongside the picture of the item, or attach a sticker that looks like a price tag.

In this game, computers can be bought for 53¢ and diamond rings for 78¢, houses for $1.21 and bicycles for 98¢...or any other prices you invent. You want the prices you come up with, however, to require combinations of coins. Unless your child is an utter neophyte at handling money, you don't want to price something at 20¢ and let her off the hook with a simple transaction of two dimes. You want her to practice combining nickels and dimes, quarters and pennies, in various combinations.

It's important for you to tell your child that these are make-believe prices and that you need hundreds or thousands of dollars to buy these things in real life.

Now the child counts out the necessary money, leaving the (hopefully) correct combination of coins on top of each picture while you go about doing something else. When she's finished, check to see if she's got all the money right.

Variations:

• Limit the child's purchasing power by purposely giving her less money than is needed for all the pictures of items you give her. Ask her which of these things she can afford to buy.

• Give her a specific challenge, such as, "Buy five of these items and have the total come as close to $5.20 as is possible."

Order in the Court(yard)

Materials: Pen or pencil, index cards

103

Order in the courtyard…and in any other part of the house you choose. Though this activity is an exercise in alphabetization, you can present it as a game to your child if you wish…or be forthright about the fact that it's an exercise in a skill, a valuable skill that too many people today grow up lacking

I've seen too many adults struggle with the phone book, unable to find the name they seek because they're not sure which comes first, "Anderson" or "Andersen," or because, faced with pages of names beginning with "P," they're absolutely buffaloed in trying to find "Peterson" and not even sure which page to start looking on.

Kids need to learn alphabetization as soon as they're old enough to spell halfway decently. And this is an exercise in that skill.

Turn your child loose in a room—or in the garden, the front yard, or even in your office, it it's a school's-out day when you've taken your child to work with you, or if you have a home office. Suggest he list every piece of furniture in the room, or everything standing on the floor, or everything visible in plain sight. (Asking him to list *everything* in the room could take days, so simplify the task by qualifying what you want him to list.) If he's in the garden, ask him to list every flower or vegetable; in the yard, it's every tree, or even *everything*—a small yard may not offer an overly generous multitude of possibilities.

He's to put each item on a separate index card, spelling it correctly (and asking you for help where necessary). Then he's to alphabetize the cards. He'll probably have no trouble putting "bed" ahead of "dresser," but if he calls a dresser a bureau, he may have to stop and think a bit about which comes first, "bed" or "bureau." And even if he knows that "paintbrush" comes ahead of "piggybank," will he know that "paintbrush" comes ahead of "paints"?

More alphabetization practice can be gotten by having your child write down all the color names he can think of—not just the basics such as "red," "blue," "green," but also "violet," "aquamarine," and "magenta," and any other Crayola-inspired or otherwise-inspired hue that occurs to him, then alphabetize them. Or he can spell out the numbers one to ten (or twenty), then put *them* in alphabetical order. It may amuse him/her that "one" is far from first, and though "ten" comes near the end, it isn't last.

If he really gets into this activity, he may be the sort who would like to keep a "card catalog" of his books. He can list each book on a card, by title and author, then alphabetize the cards, probably by title, though he might prefer to do so by author. (At this point you need to explain that, for alphabetization purposes, except in the phone book, "a" or "an" and "the" don't count. *The Secret Garden* would be alphabetized as *Secret Garden, The.*)

And of course, creating a card catalog can in turn lead to a greater pride in ownership of books, and what a good thing that is!

X Marks the Spot

Materials: Paper and pencil (with eraser)

Kids barely old enough to know their alphabet can be just as fascinated as twelve-year-olds by mapping projects, if the map is of familiar territory and not something as obscure as Europe, England, or a state halfway across the continent. Why not start with your own house?

Having your child draw a map of the house is more than just a way of passing time when your child is bored. It introduces, or reinforces, the concept of spatial relations. A surprising number of adults are unable, if asked, to tell what room is above their laundry room, or what's directly below the bedroom. If you'd take one of these people on a tour of her own house, stopping here or there and pointing up or down and asking, "What's there?" she'd for the most part be unable to tell you.

105

Many of these are the same people who don't do well with maps. Give them a map and ask them to find their way from the library to the Interstate, and a dull glaze passes over their eyes, accompanied by a confused expression.

So start your child out with a diagram of the house and work your way on to mapping out the neighborhood.

Don't give her too complex a task at first. Start by asking her to imagine she's looking down from the ceiling and to draw a picture of the room she's in, including all the furniture. If she gets that right, or at least gets the idea, you can ask her to draw the layout of the whole floor next.

You may need to help at first, and you may need to jump in from time to time with further coaching, but she ought to be able to do a fair amount of the work unaided once she gets the hang of it, allowing you to go on with whatever you were doing. You may need to start her off with a sample schematic of a house, maybe the house you grew up in, as an example. Or perhaps you'll draw the first floor of your present house and then ask her to draw the second floor.

In addition to a "map" of the house, your child can learn to draw maps of the neighborhood. Whether you draw the streets and ask your child to fill in the street names and sites of interest, or whether you ask her to draw it all herself, will depend on your child's age and whether she's had any previous exposure to mapmaking, such as in school.

If you live in the country, with long spaces between roads that are spaced at irregular intervals, the project will be more complicated, but if you live in a city, or a suburb that's laid out with streets at regular, short intervals, it should be feasible for your child to at least identify the names of the streets between your house and any location that's within walking distance, such as a friend's house, the school, the library, or the ice cream store. If none of her favorite landmarks is within walking distance, she can still fill in the names of nearby streets on the map; she ought to know, at a pretty early age, the names of the streets in your immediate vicinity.

Presented right, this activity will strike a child as a game, fun to take part in. You don't have to tell her that it's valuable practice in a skill worth learning and keeping.

Alphabet Book

Materials: Magazines, scissors, paste or glue, crayons, fifteen sheets of construction paper, stapler or paper clip

If your child is still young enough to be reading alphabet books, great. And if not, but he has a younger sibling of the right age…still great. You can ask the older child, on a day when he's bored and has no one to play with, to make the alphabet book for his younger sibling.

Either way, the method is the same: First he leafs through the magazines till he finds a picture of something beginning with an A. It could be an apple, an arm, or anything at all that's familiar. Then he cuts out the picture, gluing it onto a sheet of paper. Somewhere in the remaining space on that same page, he writes a large "A" in crayon.

Now he needs to look for a picture of a book, a ball, a bat, or some other "B" object, again cutting it out, and pasting it onto the other side of that page. Somewhere in the remaining space, he writes a large "B."

On another piece of paper, he does the same thing with "C," and of course "D" goes on the other side of that sheet. He continues that way through the alphabet, till he has all twenty-six letters represented on either side of thirteen sheets of paper. The other two sheets are the front and back covers. "_____'s Alphabet Book by [your child's name]" will look just great on the title page. If he is making it for a sibling, the sibling's name should appear in the title, with the name of the child who created the book appearing after "by."

Memorizing Instructions
Materials: Varies

This, too, is an activity that requires your participation. It's for the younger set and is not really a game, but you can make a game out of it, and at that age (mostly preschoolers), kids can have fun doing lots of things that aren't truly games.

What this really is is practice in following directions, memorizing the instructions first. Your child's nursery school or kindergarten teacher will appreciate the heck out of your instilling in your child the ability to memorize instructions and follow them, a skill a surprising number of older kids and even adults are deficient in.

Give your child a set of instructions—perhaps three or four activities—posed as a challenge ("I'll bet you can't _____" or "Can you _____?"). The activities needn't be difficult or complicated, just specific. The child needs to do each of the things you mentioned, and do them in the right order.

Your list might run, "I bet you can't crawl into your room, get a book, put it on the kitchen table, and then walk backward to the living room." Or it could be, "Can you hop on one foot to the refrigerator, do ten jumping jacks, and then fill three glasses half full of water so that the water's at the same level in all of them?"

If your child consistently succeeds at a three-"job" list, increase the list to four. If four is a breeze, give him or her five separate tasks to do. Or make each task more complicated. If your child is really young, start her out with just two tasks in tandem; work her up to three if she handles two comfortably.

Often it's difficult for a preschooler to keep several commands in her head at one time, doing each of the two, three, or four "jobs," doing them properly, doing them in the right order, and not forgetting. But with practice she'll get better at remembering what to do and doing it right.

Of course, you can use this game to sneak in an actual chore or two that needs to be done ("Put your stuffed animals in the toy chest" can be part of your list). But if a real chore is included in the list, your child may think this game is too much like work. And since the game itself is a useful learning tool, you don't want to discourage your child from wanting to play it. So it's probably best if you stick to fun assignments like hopping backward from the bed to the doorway, carrying a potato on a spoon from the kitchen to the front door, and other such silly instructions.

109

Personal Timelines

Materials: Paper and pen; optional: crayons or markers

We all know kids have trouble dealing with time concepts. To a seven-year-old, the Roaring Twenties seems as far back as the Dark Ages, and even his own personal history can tend to get muddled. But kids love talking about themselves and doing projects about themselves, and this project gets a child involved in his personal history. It clarifies just when various incidents and important markers happened to the child.

Your help is needed on this one; just how much help will depend on the age of the child. It may be sufficient for you to make a list of the years, and possibly months of those years, when key events in your child's life took place. You may need to offer more help than that, or even become fully involved in the project yourself, depending on your child's age and abilities.

He starts by drawing a long line on a long piece of paper. He labels the starting point (left side) of the line with the year he was born, and near the other end, he writes the current year (leaving room to add more data).

Now he divides the line into as many segments as he is years old, each segment of approximately equal length (it doesn't have to be precise), and labels each segment with an age. An eight-year-old would divide it into eight segments, a ten-year-old into ten segments, and so on.

In the appropriate places along the line, he fills in all the key happenings of his life. These could include: "Took my first step," "Said my first word," "Started nursery school," "Sister Jennifer born," "Brother Matt born," "Started first grade," "Started swimming lessons," "First year in Little League," "First summer at day camp," "Moved to Evanston," "Tree house built," "Learned to ride two-wheeler," and any other milestones that strike him/her as important.

Optional: Your child can illustrate some of the milestones, too, if he wants to.

Your House Is a Game Board

Materials: Your house and what's in it

There are many fun and educational activities a child can get into by herself that involve utilizing the resources available in your house. Here are just a few suggestions:

• Counting games: Ask her to count the buttons in your button box, the spoons in the drawer, the nails in the hardware cabinet, or any other item of which you have a quantity large enough to be worth counting and not so large as to frustrate the child. You can present the challenge as "We're taking inventory" (you may need to explain what an inventory is) if you wish, and ask the child to report back to you, or simply present it as an activity with no explanation needed.

Another approach to counting practice is, "Which do we have more of, forks or spoons? Screws or nails? Pots or pot covers? Sheets or towels?" This helps your child understand the concepts of more and fewer too.

• Alphabet inventories: Ask her to find one item beginning with each letter of the alphabet in her room, if she can. (To complete the inventory, it will be helpful if she has a toy xylophone, a deck of cards with a queen in it, and a stuffed zebra. Make sure she understands there are no penalties for being unable to find one item for every letter. She simply may not have something for every letter in her room, and being unable to find a "V" is not a failure.) It is perfectly acceptable for her to use one item more than once if its various parts yield different letters. For instance, a window can provide "W" (window), "G" (glass), "P" (pane), "M" (if the frames are made of metal), possibly "L" (if your windows are equipped with locks), and maybe even "S" (streaks).

Next ask her to do the same thing around the rest of the house, searching out an "A," a "B," a "C," and so forth in the other rooms.

Now ask her whether there are more "G" or "B" items in the house (or any other two letters you think she can find a good quantity of items for).

You may need to set down special rules for the game if needed: No going into sister's drawers, no going into brother's room, no going into Dad's toolbox.

• The next challenge can be to find items around the house that resemble letters. This will be harder, but surely there are a few L-, I-, H-, and O-shaped objects...and the longer it takes the child to find such items, the longer she's kept busy, as long as the search isn't so hard as to prove frustrating.

• For the older child, if you happen to have squares of tiles in the kitchen, bathroom, hallway, laundry room, or anywhere else (including the bathroom walls), multiplication practice is at hand if you ask her to tell you how many tiles there are on the wall, in the hall, or wherever without counting each tile, just by counting across and down, then multiplying. *Then* have her count them all to see if she got the correct answer. (If that sounds too much like homework rather than fun, offer a reward for a correct answer...no cheating and no fudging, though.)

• Find objects around the house and ask the child how

many uses she can think of for each one. A wooden spoon, a pot, the bathtub, a rag, a sheet, a cardboard box. The uses don't have to be supersensible; let her fancy run free. Praise creative suggestions rather than belittling them as impractical, even if you do point out the impracticalities of them.
• The Chore Chase: For this one you need a floor with tiles on it, a penny or playing piece from a game, and a young child who has a few small chores you'd like her to do before dinner (or lunch or bedtime or some other definable limit). Give your child a list—written or oral—of the chores you want done, making it a reasonable number of things for her to accomplish in the time allowed. Define a "finish line"—a wall or doorway is fine—and place the penny or playing piece the same number of squares away from that finish line as the number of chores that are on your list.

Your challenge to your child is to see if she can get the playing piece to the finish line by dinnertime. Every time she accomplishes one of the items on your list, she moves the playing piece one square farther along toward the finish line. If she gets all the chores done, the playing piece will come to rest in the doorway, at the wall, or whatever. If this happens before you call dinner, she has won.

The smaller the child, the less likely you'll get the question "What do I win?" Winning will be enough of an accomplishment without there being a reward. An older child is more likely to want a tangible reward for succeeding. If you don't play the game every night and don't make the reward too large, there's no harm in a little mild bribery.

113

Those are just a few ways to utilize your house as a game board. Look around, see what your resources are, and think of the possibilities. Invent games using the items found around your house. Your imagination is the only limit.

Introducing You To...

Materials: Crayons or markers and paper to draw on, pen or pencil and paper to write on

This fun activity involves both drawing and writing and gets kids' creative juices flowing. It's also good practice for any child who is interested in creative writing.

Start by asking the child to draw a picture of any person of any age—not a real person, nor a person from a book or TV, but a person he's invented out of his own head. It could be a man, woman, boy, or girl, or even a visitor from another planet.

Now have your child write down some information about this person. It doesn't have to be in story form. We're not looking for a whole story about this person, but rather for data about them. We can see what color hair and eyes they have, from the drawing, but how tall a person is this? How much do they weigh? How old are they? If an adult, what kind of work do they do? If a college or high school student, what are they studying? If a younger child, what school do they go to and what are their favorite classes?

Regardless of age, what are this person's hobbies? Favorite foods? Favorite kind of music? Favorite animals? The more information your child comes up with, the better. He needn't stop with the questions I've just posed; let him come up with as much more information as he can.

What are the person's pet hates, favorite things, and funny personality quirks? What are their favorite sayings? Favorite foods? Favorite animals? Do they have any pets? Do they have any odd habits?

If your child really gets into this, he can go on, making up such information as the person's most embarrassing moment, their happiest Christmas memory, what they like to do with their friends, and any other traits or quirks.

Of course, if he wants, your child can write a whole story about the person. But even if he never writes the story, just inventing the details that make the person come to life is an activity that will at the very least help develop that most-needed "muscle," the imagination. It will also aid the child if he has any aspirations to being a writer. And, last but far from least, it can occupy a goodly chunk of his time on an afternoon when he's at a loss for something to do.

"Photo Opportunities"

We know what a "photo opportunity" is to a politician posing for the cameras at a fortuitous time. But you don't have to be a politician or a photojournalist to enjoy these "photo opportunities"—just a kid. Anytime a child is looking for something to do, photographs will present an opportunity to have fun.

These activities all involve photos, some of them magazine or newspaper photos, some of them photos your family took, many of them discards. So stop throwing out those pictures that don't quite come out right. Your child's about to get busy and have fun with them—and you, too, will have fun with the results.

These Balloons Don't Fly

Materials: Pictures (either photos or newspaper or magazine pictures), white paper, scissors, glue or paste, pen

A balloon is not only a colorful thing you inflate with air or helium and tie off; "balloon" is also the name given to the white space with writing in it that floats above a cartoon character's head and tells what he is saying (or thinking).

Your child can have fun with photos slated for the discard pile, or with magazine or newspaper pictures (pictures from ads are fine for this, too), adding balloons to the pictures and putting words in the mouths of the people pictured.

All she has to do is cut out a few circles or ovals of suitable sizes, each with a little tail hanging down, in the manner of a comic strip balloon. (If she's never paid attention to the balloons before, let her open the paper to the comic page for a minute and take note of how it's done.)

Now she sifts through the photos or magazine or newspaper pictures on hand. If she tries to think of funny things the people pictured might be saying, ideas will come to mind. When an idea strikes, she picks a suitably sized balloon, writes the words on the balloon, and pastes it onto the picture.

These balloons don't fly, but they're lots of fun all the same.

Newspaper Capers

Materials: Newspaper, eraser, pencil or pen

Hours of giggling creativity are available to your child with no more special equipment than an old newspaper, an eraser, and a pencil or pen.

An eraser will easily rub out a part of a newspaper photo. (Faces lend themselves best to this activity as a rule.) The child can erase the whole face, or just a portion of it—say, the nose, the mouth, or one eye. The he replaces it with one of his own devising.

How about furnishing ferocious, Groucho-style eyebrows to the meek, mild face of a small-featured man? What about drawing an impossibly huge mouth on the face of a pretty women? Or get into political satire just a bit...how about drawing in a Pinocchio-style long nose on the face of the ex-president who once promised "No new taxes" and then imposed some?

Does a recent picture show the local kennel club's winner? How about erasing the dog's tail and replacing it with something somewhat simian? Or if not an ape's tail on a dog, how about the eight tentacles of an octopus in lieu of a bird's legs?

Related activity: Your child—especially if he's older and reasonably clever—can have similar fun by erasing a caption beneath a newspaper photo and substituting a caption of his own. Again, as above, the captions can be political or just plain silly. A local official known for prevarication, holding up a plaque (perhaps actually proclaiming a site to be of historical importance, or something equally innocuous), might have the following caption appended: "Councilman receives Liar-of-the-Month

Plaque." But for a six-year-old, it might be funny to erase the caption beneath a photo of a scientist gazing skyward with a telescope and replace it with "Dr. X looks for lost dog" or "Dr. X searches for his supper." It may not be the funniest thing you've ever read, but to a six-year-old....

Whether your child is a twelve-year-old creating political satire or a six-year-old just being silly, either way, he's going to be having fun.

Homemade Jigsaw Puzzles

Materials: Color pictures cut from magazines, lightweight cardboard or similar (old file folders are great for this), pencil, glue or paste, scissors

Here's an activity that your child can engage in as a solo amusement and that will in turn provide the child with yet another activity to do by herself!

With just the items listed above, she can create a jigsaw puzzle herself that's pleasing to her eye, as easy or difficult as she wishes, and fun to make.

Searching through an old magazine, she finds a large picture that appeals to her. It could be scenic, an animal, kids at play, a shiny new car, or any other picture she finds appealing. It may happen to be part of an advertisement—that's okay, though it's certainly preferable that no words of advertising appear within the picture itself.

After carefully cutting it out, she pastes or glues it to a piece of lightweight cardboard or similar. If the picture is smaller than the cardboard, she now needs to trim the cardboard to match. Then she cuts the picture, now attached to the cardboard, in a jigsaw pattern.

She may want to figure out just what sort of pattern she wants to use in cutting before actually using the scissors. This can be accomplished by drawing the pattern on the reverse side of the cardboard. If she uses a pencil, she can erase and redraw the lines till she's satisfied. If she's supremely confident, she can skip the drawing, though, and just cut freehand.

Either way, with or without pencil guidelines, she cuts the picture. If she's making the puzzle for a young brother or sister, she might want to cut it in something like six large, simple pieces. But assuming it's for herself, she should cut a reasonable number of pieces, as complicated as she can stand without exceeding her frustration tolerance level. This may be one hundred small, twisty, curvy, complex pieces, or something considerably simpler.

Your child now has a jigsaw puzzle that she will enjoy all the more because she chose the picture herself and because she created the puzzle herself too.

Another source of pictures for jigsaw puzzles is Christmas cards. Some have very pretty scenes on them. If yours is not a family that saves Christmas cards, consider letting your child cut the most scenic ones up for jigsaw puzzles. Since the cards are printed on heavier stock, most don't need to be backed on cardboard. They won't be as durable as commercial jigsaw puzzles, but considering that they cost exactly nothing and that they can be replaced easily by cutting up another card, durability is not a great factor.

As Christmas cards are smaller than the typical jigsaw puzzle, your child will want to cut small pieces to maintain the complexity of the puzzle.

Another possibility is for your child to draw or paint a picture herself, then back that picture with cardboard and cut it up in the manner I've just described.

Uncle Allan's in Pieces!
Materials: Photographs, scissors; optional: pencil

If your child is into jigsaw puzzles, and you've got photos that didn't come out right, you've got a perfect match. Instead of discarding that picture in which the tree seems to be growing out of Dad's head, or little Annie was sticking her tongue out at the camera, give it to your child to cut up and turn into a jigsaw puzzle.

Unless the picture is quite large, he'll have to cut small pieces. This is done more easily with a small scissors, though it's not impossible with a large one. He may wish to plan ahead by drawing the cut lines on the back of the photo with a pencil, though this is not necessary.

The advantage to drawing the lines first is obvious: He can design what seems like a good series of cuts, erasing and starting over if need be, and not cutting till he's sure he has it the way he wants it. On the other hand, the disadvantage is that he can't see where on the picture the cut lines are falling. Should he want to be sure that the face is cut in half, or that it's left intact, or that a cut falls in a certain place, he has no assurance that the lines he's drawing on the back will fall where he wants on the picture.

One other alternative is to draw the cut lines on a piece of thin tissue paper laid over the photo, but now we're getting unnecessarily complicated. This is supposed to be fun, not work.

When the photo is in pieces, your child can try to put it back together again. If it's too easy, he'll know that next time he needs to cut smaller pieces and in a more complicated pattern. Throw the picture out and start over with a fresh one. Don't worry about using up too many pictures. They were discards anyway. Have fun!

Magazine Picture Scavenger Hunt

Materials: Magazines, scissors, list provided by you

Prepare this activity for your child ahead of time by making up a list of twenty items that can be found pictured in an assortment of magazines. (If you have only one or two magazines available for cutting up, you may want to do a little prep work by looking in the magazines and seeing what's pictured in them.) Make sure the child understands she's free to cut pictures from ads as well as article illustrations.

A sample list of items might be:

Pen
Red car
Cat
Two-story house
Store
Inside of office
Tall building
Bicycle
Boat
Soap
Hammer
Golf club

"Photo Opportunities"

People playing a game
Someone fishing
Table with food on it
Glass with something in it
Sunglasses
Hand with at least one ring on a finger
Moving van
Pair of shorts

How your list will read is going to depend on what magazines you've got available. Obviously if you have mostly sports magazines, mostly homemaking magazines, or mostly business magazines, that's going to affect what pictures you're going to send your child searching for.

You can set your child a time limit or leave the game open-ended. You can award her a prize for finding all the items and being "a winner," or simply say "That's very good!" and reward her with praise but nothing more concrete if she succeeds.

Either way, you're the real winner, because she's going to be occupied for a while, and you won't have to listen to, "Mommy, I'm bored. There's no one to play with."

Magazine Letter
Scavenger Hunt
Materials: Magazines, scissors, list provided by you

Akin to Magazine Picture Scavenger Hunt, above, and also a "cousin" to Alphabet Book (page 107), this activity will have your child looking through magazines to find pictures of items beginning with various letters of the alphabet.

Kids who are too old to make an alphabet book for themselves (and have no younger sibling to make one for) will have no objection to going on a scavenger hunt through magazines for items beginning with certain letters. Finding pictures for the whole alphabet at one time may be too time-consuming an undertaking for their attention spans and seem too much like a chore. Certain letters are difficult to find pictures for anyhow—how many magazines have pictures of xylophones or zoos? Even Queen Elizabeth doesn't get pictured terribly often.

But you can easily give a child a list of ten or fifteen letters—excluding those tricky ones, unless you're aware that one of the magazines you're about to hand over contains a picture of a zither, or a feature on the San Diego Zoo.

Tell your child that to complete the scavenger hunt, he needs to find a picture of an object that begins with each of the letters on your list. He can, of course, accomplish much with pictures of people; the various body parts alone can account for lots of letters, and items of clothing will help with the rest (arm, body, cheeks, dress, ears, face, gums, hair...you get the idea). But unless your child is getting too frustrated trying to find suitable pictures, you might not want to make it *that* easy and can refrain from pointing out the multiple possibilities inherent in one picture of a person.

You may want to point out, though, that some pictures can represent multiple letters of the alphabet. For instance, a picture of a car can be used for "A" (automobile), "C" (car), "S" (sedan), or "H" (hardtop) or "C" again (convertible). Moreover, the various visible parts of the car (hood, windshield, fender, bumper, trunk, etc.) can represent different letters of the alphabet, according to what's needed.

By varying the letters you challenge your child to find, and by giving him different magazines to cut up, you can keep this activity fresh from one time to the next, so your child won't tire of it quickly.

Photo Finish

Materials: Photo album, paper, pen

It's always fun to look through photo albums and remember the events surrounding the pictures...when you can. But what of that picture of Sean in the Indian headdress, looking about seven or nine years old...just where was that taken? And how old was he, exactly? Funny, how the things you think will be so important turn out to be less remember-able than you'd thought.

Even Sean may forget after a while. He may be sure it wasn't taken in camp or at Scouts, yet forget where it *was* taken. Or he may remember *where* it was taken but forget the circumstances surrounding it.

Ideally, photos should capture more than just the way your child (or whoever is the subject) looked in a given year. They should, at least wherever applicable, capture a memory, a story surrounding the picture.

"Oh, I remember when that picture of you with the kitten was taken. You were six years old and you'd just found the kitten under the azalea bush. It had wandered away from Mrs. Rodgers, but you didn't know that yet. You were heartbroken to find it belonged to someone; you wanted to keep it. Mrs. Rodgers gave you a big piece of pie and said you'd done your good deed for the day, but you cried 'cause you couldn't keep the kitten."

But what if you *don't* remember the story of the kitten...or why Billy is scowling so intently at the fire truck in this picture, or who the girl is that Sara has her arm around in this picture.

Quick! Before the kids' memories evaporate, too, get them each to look through the family photo albums and write up a little paragraph or two to go with every picture they remember the circumstances surrounding. This is an activity that's best done by one child at a time, turning the pages at her own rate of speed and writing brief histories for each picture she can identify. So even if you're a multichild family, this is best done as an activity for one child. Let each take a turn with the book.

Two-page essays on each picture are not what's called for here, though something more than a one-line caption is in order when possible. A few sentences should be enough to capture the essence of the story behind each picture.

128

Of course, some kids are more loquacious than others, and some are natural writers. If your child does tend to get lengthy in her explanations, that's fine. Just don't put her off from participating in this project by making your child feel as if the photo album is an essay test.

There will be some pictures for which no explanation is forthcoming. The child may not remember the circumstances behind the picture. Or the circumstances may have more to do with the photographer than with the child—Dad had just gotten a new camera, but it was an ordinary day in the child's life. Or the occasion for the picture was a visit from relatives or some other such event that was meaningful to you but not to the child.

But encourage your child to write up the story behind the picture wherever possible. She may think she'll always remember the last picnic with her best friend Julia before she moved to Wyoming, but childhood evanesces, and so do memories.

Get it down in writing, before it's lost to all of you. Half the value of those pictures in the album is the stories they evoke. Wouldn't it be a shame to lose those precious memories?

Picturing a Childhood

Materials: Photo album, photos, pen and paper

Of course, *you* have a family photo album, with pictures of your child as well as other family photos. But why shouldn't your child have a photo album to keep for himself...complete with captions or maybe even longer commentary?

This is an activity that can't be done all at once. Whenever he has some free time, and the inclination to work on his album, he can put in a little work at a time. Gradually he'll get it together...though even then it won't be completed, because he'll add to it as time goes by.

The bare-bones format would simply be an album with photos in it. These would certainly include photos of the child, as taken by you, and might include photos of others (certainly you!) that the child would like to include. If the child has a camera, he'll want to include photos he himself has taken, along with the ones of him.

For the photos of the child, you can certainly part with some of the ones you've taken, without having to order duplicates of good pictures. If you take a roll of only twelve shots, have two kids, and get six shots of each, you're not going to need all six shots for your own album. You'll probably choose one or two for your album, sending another one or two off to the grandparents. This still leaves two or more for the child. Every time you take a roll of photos, you can offer your child the "leftover shots" of himself.

129

Taking this activity one step further, your child can caption each of the photos with a little label. (Though he can use an actual press-on label for this, a small piece of paper works fine too.) A simple caption could read "At Camp Pine Bough, 1994, with bunkmates in Bunk Cherokee" or "Fourth grade, Eisenhower Elementary, 1995."

But if he wants, your child can get even more elaborate, writing as long a description he wants about the circumstances surrounding each picture. Insert the paragraph or page—he can make it as long as he wants—into the album at the appropriate point. Number the photo, and number the descriptive writing with the corresponding number. (There might be six photos of each of two facing pages when you open the book at random. If each gets a paragraph, you're going to need to know which paragraph refers to which picture.) If there are so many written descriptions that you don't have room for all the written pages between the pages of photos, keep the written pages out of the album but keep them together, and keep them together with the album.

Now when your child looks back at his age-seven photos from the vantage point of a fourteen-year-old, he won't have to ask, "Mom, where was this taken? Why was I wearing an Indian headdress? Who's the guy sitting on the tree stump?" He'll have the answers to all those questions...and in his own words.

Mixed-Media Art

Materials: Photos that would otherwise have been discarded, pictures cut from magazines, construction paper, glue or paste, scissors, and possibly crayons or paints

These pictures are fun to create because they're more creative than the average childhood art, involving different media and more planning ahead than the average picture. They're also a great idea for kids who like to create art but can't draw a simple dog that's recognizable from a dinosaur.

First the child needs to assemble her materials. Start with photos that would otherwise have been discarded. If Mom came out great in this one but Dad was squinting, and you don't want it for the family album, don't toss it. It will find a home in a mixed-media picture.

After studying the resources at hand—the available photos and also magazine pictures—your child needs to think…what can she create from the "ingredients" at hand? Here are examples: Your child has a photo of Dad throwing a ball at little brother Timmy. Your child also has a magazine picture of batting great Bobby Bonds at bat. The two men's pictures are relatively similar in size. (This is important.) The child cuts carefully around each picture, cutting out Dad and the ball, also Bobby Bonds and his bat, discarding the rest of each picture.

Now she pastes the two men's pictures off to opposite sides of a sheet of construction paper. It appears that Dad is pitching to Bobby Bonds! Of course one is clearly cut from a photo and the other from a magazine picture. You're not attempting to fool anyone with the picture. But that is the effect.

Other bits can be added to the picture from other cutouts. They may blend seriously or humorously with the basic part of the picture. They might include a cartoon drawing of the sun smiling as it casts its rays down. Or a magazine photo of a man in a lounge chair, sipping an iced tea and sunbathing, wryly observing the pitch-and-bat action. Or a picture of a stand full of cheering fans.

Let's take another example. A picture of Mom, cut out of an old photo, is pasted on construction paper. A bouquet of flowers is cut out of a magazine and placed in her hand. A crown from yet another magazine picture is placed on her head.

If a key ingredient for a proposed picture can't be found in any magazine or photo, it can be drawn or painted onto the picture. Got a picture of sister Caitlin and a magazine picture of a ferocious lion? Great...but where's the whip for Caitlin's hand? It can be crayoned or painted in. Or your child can cut the shape of a whip out of a piece of brown construction paper and paste that in.

The tricky part of these pictures is to find elements that match each other reasonably closely in size. If the photo of Dad your child cuts out is taller than the house picture she cuts from a magazine, she'd better keep looking for a different house picture...or paste the house near the top of the page in a way that suggests it's way in the distance and only *appears* smaller than Dad.

But this is one type of art that requires creativity and imagination more than the usual type of artistic abilities. If your child can't draw a straight line, she can skip the drawing or painting aspect of a mixed-media picture and stick to cut-and-paste with very respectable results.

Photo Collages

Materials: Construction paper, cardboard, glue, scissors, old photos

Here's another use for extra photos and photos in which one person came out great but another didn't. Got three similar pictures of the family picnicking at the pier, and you really need only one for the family album? Got a picture in which Dad looks fine but Becky's eyes are closed? What you've got is the materials for a photo collage.

Here's how your child goes about making one: Start by gluing a piece of construction paper (black, white, or pastel) to a piece of cardboard. (For an extra-large piece of cardboard, use more than one piece of same-colored construction paper.) Now cut up the photos. In most cases he'll want to cut out carefully around the people, discarding the background and saving only the person's picture. In some cases, he may want just the head, or head and shoulders, or head and upper body, rather than the whole body. (In some cases the whole body won't be in the picture to begin with.)

Artistically arrange the photos on the construction paper. It's okay for one photo to overlap part of another. When he's satisfied with the arrangement, he applies glue and glues the photos in place. If desired, he can cut out a brown "frame" of construction paper and paste it in place on top of the background construction paper.

Variation—Comic Collage:
Your child can also make a collage out of cutouts of his favorite comic book characters. The procedure is essentially the same. I'd suggest a white background in this case, though.

The Missing Half

Materials: One large color picture of a face cut from a magazine (an advertisement is okay), crayons, scissors, glue or paste, large piece of white paper

Find a large color picture of someone's face in a magazine and cut it out. Now cut the picture in half from top to bottom, so you have only the left or right side of the picture. Paste or glue the picture to the white paper.

Now your child's objective is to draw on the white paper, with crayons, the missing half of the picture. She should try to make her half resemble the original half as closely as possible, in terms of skin tone, eye color, hair color, and lip tone, as well as the shape of the nose, eyes, lips, ears, etc.

The results are likely to prove amusing.

Mixies

Materials: Old magazines, scissors, cardboard, glue or paste

For this fun game, you or the child need to prepare by cutting out photos from magazines. The requirements for these photos are that they be full-length shots, approximately the same size as each other, and of recognizable "types," rather than generic people.

Ideally you'd like something along the lines of the following mix: a football player, a construction worker, a uniformed nurse, a uniformed police officer, a typical grandmotherly type, a typical teen, and other identifiable types—the more, the merrier.

134

If you can't find one of each of the types I've suggested, don't fret, but do look for as many different recognizable occupations, types, uniforms, etc., as you can. You want some men and some women; it doesn't matter how many of each, or whether your doctor, nurse, construction worker, businessperson, and others are men or women.

Now you or your child pastes each picture on cardboard. It is preferable but not necessary to then cut around the photo so you have a cutout of the figure with no cardboard showing. It *is* necessary to cut each figure twice—once at the neck and once at the waist.

Here's where the child's fun starts. He plays Mixies by mixing the different heads together, and the bodies, and the legs. Then he assembles them by placing a head over a body over legs...but not the original head, body, and legs that go together. Instead, he may choose to put the head of a nurse, complete with cap, over the body of a police officer, complete with uniform, over the legs of a Radio City Rockette doing high kicks, or the face of a football player, complete with helmet, over the body of a basketball player, including uniform and holding the basketball, over the stockinged and high-heel-clad legs of a woman banker.

Young kids can have fun with Mixies, combining picture after ludicrous picture, turning out results that will have the rest of the family giggling too.

Miscellaneous Activities

A potpourri of pleasures, this section contains diverse activities. Some are active, some quiet; some are creative or thought-provoking, some just for fun. Whatever your child's interests or personality, you're sure to find activities in this section that she'll get into with enthusiasm. And some, like Cardboard Dollhouses, Kiddie City, or My Memory Book, will leave her with a finished product that will entertain her on lots of subsequent occasions.

"Ransom" Stories

Materials: Magazines, scissors, paste or glue, paper

You know how the classic ransom note is written—at least in literature. The words are cut out of magazine pages, one word at a time, and pasted down on a sheet of paper. Your child can write a short story the same way, cutting one word at a time from magazines, then pasting the words onto a sheet of paper.

The words can come from stories, titles, ads, or anywhere else. Magazines are preferable to newspapers as newsprint is so messy to work with. Your child can either decide on a story ahead of time, or scan the assortment of words in front of him and make up the story as he goes along in accordance with the words that are available.

He should not cut whole paragraphs or sentences out. Each word should be cut out by itself, each word of the story coming from somewhere else in the magazine. It's more fun (and more traditional) to use large print, such as you'd find in ads and titles, than to use the small print you'd find within the text of a story. But if words found in small-print text are needed, there's no real reason not to use them.

The stories, of necessity, are going to be very short and not very literary. The fun is in cutting and pasting, and in looking at them; you cannot judge them on their merit *as stories*. Your child will simply have fun putting one of these stories together, seeing what he can devise in the way of a plot with just the elements at hand.

Do the characters live "happily ever after"? You'll have to read to the end to find out. No fair skipping ahead!

Dry-Land Fishing

Materials: Large pan (such as roasting or dishwashing pan); stick or twig about 1 foot long, or ruler (foot, not yardstick); string (about 1 foot long); bobby pin or hairpin; hole punch; paper or (preferably) cardboard; scissors; crayons or paint

It won't matter if it's raining or freezing out, and you'll never be bitten by mosquitoes. Dry-land fishing is an all-weather sport and definitely an indoor sport as well...though there's nothing to prevent your young angler from doing her fishing in your backyard if that's what suits her.

140

You also won't have to clean the fish your child catches, as they're made of cardboard or paper. Definitely not "keepers," these fish are meant to be thrown back time after time.

In fact, before she engages in any fishing, your child needs to first create the fish. This is done by cutting them out of paper or, even better, cardboard, in varying sizes in a suggested range of from two inches to six inches. They can be painted or crayoned, and the wilder the colors, the more attractive they'll be to catch. Why fish for trout when you can catch exotic tropicals, or even fish such as never existed anywhere on this planet?

With a hole punch, punch a hole near the mouth of each fish.

The ruler, stick, or twig is the fishing pole, with the length of string tied to it. Separate the two halves of a bobby pin or hairpin. Tie the end of the string to one half, and bend the other into a hook. Dump the fish into the pan, and your angler is ready to see if they're biting at the local fishing hole—right in her own room, or the living room or family room.

She won't need a fishing license to go after these beauties, she won't need any help when she hooks a big one, and perhaps best of all, there's no chance she'll fall in and get wet.

Friend-Ships

Materials: Wood pieces; small jar with tight-fitting lid; small evergreen branches, wildflowers, or dandelions; glue; saw or nails; paper and indelible pen and pencil; proximity to river or lake; optional: short, fat candles and matches

A Friend-Ship floats out of your child's life and hopefully into the life of a new friend. It's constructed of wood and wishes. Unless your child is old enough to use a saw or nails responsibly, some parental participation is called for with the wood.

The "ship" can be merely a raft—all it has to be is something large enough to hold a jar, perhaps a few candles, and perhaps some decorations. If you have one perfect-sized piece of wood, your child doesn't need to do any sawing or nailing. But if the only wood you have around the house is a large, unwieldy piece, someone's going to need to cut it down. And if all you have is too-small scraps, someone's going to need to nail two or three of them together.

Next your child needs to glue the jar to the middle of the "ship." Center it carefully so that it won't cause the ship to tilt and capsize. Now he needs to write a note that hopefully will reach another child. In it he should introduce himself: name, age, address, and interests. If he has an ambiguous, unisex name and his interests don't make it clear which sex he is, it might be good to specify that too.

The note goes into the jar, with the lid going on securely

tightly afterward. But just in case of leakage, the note should be written in either pencil or indelible ink so that it won't run in case of mishap.

One or more short, fat candles (lower center of gravity) can be attached to the ship if it's to be set afloat at night. For a daytime launch, or if the child is too young to handle fire responsibly and no parent will be around for the launch, or if dry weather conditions make a burning candle a fire hazard when the ship reaches the other shore, skip the candles.

The ship can be decorated with small evergreen branches, with wildflowers, clover, or dandelions, or left plain.

Now all that remains is for the child to take the friend-ship to a shoreline—of a river or lake, not the ocean!—and launch it. Will a comparably aged child of the same sex and compatible interests find it? Will that child and your child become great friends? Or will the ship be found be someone living far enough away that only a pen-pal friendship is possible?

If the ship never gets into friendly hands, your child can always build another friend-ship and try again.

Circus Train

Materials: At least three shoeboxes (without lids), paint or crayons, yarn, sharp implement such as scissors that parent can use to punch holes in boxes, toy animals

Little ones can have a good time pulling this "circus train" around the house, but parental help will be needed in creating it. Each shoebox is going to be one car of the circus train, which your youngster can paint to look realistic (or you can help her). Depending on the appearance of the shoeboxes, she may need to paint over the writing on each shoebox first with a solid coat of a light-colored paint before painting Jenny's Circus or mock bars on each car.

For the lead car and each of the middle cars of the train (on a three-car train, there will only be one middle car, of course), punch one hole at either end, low on the box and centered in the middle. For the last car, you only need one hole. Thread a length of yarn about 12 inches through the hole of the lead car. Knot the end of the yarn inside the box, to keep the yarn from slipping out. Now thread a length of yarn about eight inches through the back of that car and the front of the next car, knotting each end inside its box so that the yarn is secure. Repeat till all the cars are linked.

Your child can now put small toy animals inside the cars and pretend they're circus animals, pulling the train around. Small plastic or rubber figures work better than stuffed animals in that they're a better size to fit in the shoeboxes. If your child doesn't have any suitably sized animals, she can always cut pictures out of magazines or draw animals on paper or cardboard.

143

Squirt-a-Cup

Materials: Squirt gun, small cup

This is not the most sophisticated of solitaire games...but then, doesn't that make it perfect for the average, basically silly child? It's not educational either...though it *is* cooling on a hot summer's day! And a substantial amount of time can be passed in this activity on that hot, lazy afternoon.

The object of the game is simply to transfer the contents of a squirt gun into a small cup—over and over, till the cup is filled.

The smaller the cup, the better; you'll be surprised how many pulls of a squirt-gun trigger it takes to fill even a small cup.

Of course, the child can stand in front of the cup and fire point-blank at it. That's fun enough. But trick shots are lots more fun! Over-the-shoulder and between-the-legs at a cup on the ground behind him are two possible trick shots; let him think of others. Blindfolded? Point-blank after spinning around five times quickly?

If your child is a statistics freak, the kind who's seriously into record keeping (and we do know children like that!), he may get into keeping track of how many squirt-gun-fuls it takes to fill the cup—or to fill each of several different cups, or to fill the cup during various tricky maneuvers.

144

But keeping track is by no means necessary on any level, even mentally. This needn't be any kind of contest, a try-to-top-last-round performance. Just ready, aim, fire, have fun!

How Do You Get to Carnegie Hall?

Materials: Varies

Remember the old joke? A lost tourist in New York approaches a local resident on the street and inquires, "How do you get to Carnegie Hall?" The New Yorker answers, "Practice, practice, practice."

Point well taken. The way to get ahead in *anything* is to practice and perfect your skills...and that applies to softball and chess as much as to piano or violin virtuosity.

If you have a child with time on her hands who's looking for something to do, suggest she practice. "Practice" doesn't have to mean repetitive exercises of something the child considers a chore or a bore. It doesn't have to mean sitting at the piano and playing scales... though it certainly could mean that if your child is "taking" piano and wants to improve.

It could also mean going to the local ball field, if it's within walking or biking distance, and practicing pitching from a not-in-current-use pitcher's mound. It could mean setting up the chess board and experimenting with different openings. It could mean, in fact, improving at any skill or talent the child has, or any game or sport the child would like to be better at.

"Practice" has such a ring of drudgery, doesn't it? It rates right up there with "homework" on the Dreaded Words List. But it doesn't need to. Rather than think of it as a chore, as work, as something to be avoided, your child should think of it as a way of getting better at an activity she enjoys, or a way of improving her skills at a game or sport she's not as good at as she'd like to be.

So don't you present the suggestion in a way that makes it sound like a chore. Saying "Why not brush up on your football?" might come out sounding more appealing than "Why don't you practice?"

And by the way, there's no rule that says "All football practicing has to be done between August and January." If your child needs a little practice in kicking a football to hone his accuracy, he can do this in April or June, too. ("Think how much better at it you'll be when football season comes around again," you might suggest.) The same goes for practicing pitching in any weather that doesn't involve striving for throwing accuracy while wearing a ski jacket and gloves.

If your child is a young golfer, she can practice putting in the backyard by setting up two blocks (or any similar markers) about

145

as far apart from each other as the width of a hole in golf, then trying to putt the ball between the blocks from various spots around the yard.

While pitching is best practiced in a ball field or a city park or playground, it can also be practiced in your yard if you have a particularly large one, with no windows—yours or the neighbors'—in range of stray pitches. Ditto batting. Kids have been throwing the ball up in the air to self-pitch for batting practice from time immemorial. And a modicum of batting expertise can be obtained by practicing with a rubber ball and a broom handle—far less dangerous to nearby windows, and if a child can hit a ball with that narrow broom handle, she'll have a much better chance at connecting with a much wider baseball or softball bat.

Yes, the child will have to chase her own pitched or batted balls, kicked footballs, served volleyballs, kicked soccer balls, etc., but if she's been watching lots of TV lately, it'll do her some good to get the exercise she's been missing.

And "practice" doesn't have to mean sports any more than it has to mean a musical instrument. Your child can practice new chess openings, or any other game—board game, electronic game, paper-and-pen game, or other—that one can get better at playing by sharpening one's skills.

Your kid might become a major league pitcher, a violin virtuoso, the neighborhood paper-airplane champion, the local penny-pitching whiz, or simply a better hopscotch player.

How do you get to Carnegie Hall?

Sears, Roebuck, & Annie

Materials: Paper, pen, possibly crayons or markers, stapler, items your child is ready to get rid of

In the old days it was lemonade stands, at which not only lemonade but often used comics or even used toys were sold. But the trend today in sales to adult consumers is toward mail-order merchandising, and as adults go, so goes the younger set.

The old Sears catalog is no more, but a profusion of others, many of them more narrow in their appeal, clog the mailboxes of homes across America. You may enjoy reading them, or you may curse the clutter. Regardless of your reaction, your child is quite possibly a catalog reader, even if he's never ordered a toy or other treasure from one. Most kids are fascinated by catalogs—such an array of interesting items, intriguing pictures, many of them in color.

147

But why not take it one step further? Rather than just being a reader of catalogs, why doesn't your child "publish" one…and put in it all those used comics, outgrown books, and gently used toys that no longer hold his interest? If he could sell them—even for a dime or a quarter each—he'd be ahead of the game, and so would you with fewer items to clutter his room!

The child who can't be persuaded to give away outgrown boxed games, stuffed toys, or similar, no matter how worthwhile the charity or how needy the family toward which you're trying to steer the items, will do a 180-degree turnabout regarding divesting himself of old belongings if he smells money in the exchange.

If you or the child will fold five or six pieces of typing paper in half and staple two or three times along the fold, he'll have the pages he can transform into a catalog of items for sale. Using a pen (or pencil), he now writes the name of each of the items he wishes to sell, along with a brief description of each and the price he wishes to get for each. (Some consultation with you is in order here. You may also wish to consult on the items to be disposed of, to make sure you approve and nothing vital, or in the nature of a family heirloom, is going out the door.)

Your child can make the items more appealing by drawing a picture of each. (That's where the crayons or markers come into the picture.) But if he has no faith in his artistic ability, a good description of each item should be sufficient.

Unlike grown-up catalogs, your child's catalog doesn't have to be duplicated and mailed out. He can show around his one copy to friends and schoolmates, taking orders from the catalogue or bringing specified items to school to show would-be buyers who are interested but want to see the merchandise in person.

Kiddie City

Materials: Large sheet of plastic, permanent marker, building blocks; optional: small toy cars, small toy people or dolls, small toy buildings

This activity requires some preparation by you, but the time is worth it as the payoff is hours of involved fun on the part of your child. You'll need a large sheet of fairly durable plastic. You can buy an edged tarp, a roll of storm-window material, or a paint store dropcloth. Canvas works here, too, though it's bulkier to store. In a pinch, an old bedsheet (pale, solid color) will even do.

Whatever material you wind up using, it will be the basis for your child's city.

The size of the city—the size of the plastic—is going to depend on the area you have available for your child to lay it out in. If you have an attic, basement, or playroom with a large expanse of unoccupied floor, you might even want to let your child have a city that's 8 by 10 feet. If not, choose a smaller expanse of plastic.

Laying out the street grids is your job. Using a thick-tipped permanent marker, draw streets directly on the plastic. Make the scale fairly large. Streets aren't a single line but are spaces between parallel lines approximately eight inches apart. Make the intersections open—an intersection should look like a cross, not like a tic-tac-toe board, so plan ahead.

Once you've laid the streets out, it's your child's turn to go to work constructing the city. If she wants, she can use building blocks, Legos, or similar items to construct the buildings. If she has toy houses or other buildings from games on hand and wants to incorporate them into the city, and they're in approximately the right scale for the city, fine. Similarly, the inhabitants of the city can be appropriate-sized dolls or action figures, toy people from a game, or paper cutouts, or they can be totally imaginary inhabitants. Correctly scaled toy cars or trucks can serve as the vehicles that drive the streets of Kiddie City (or Marystown, Charlieville, etc.).

Another way of populating the city is with pictures of people cut from magazines, and those same magazines can provide the cars, buildings, and even street lights if your child is seriously deficient in building blocks. But if your child has building blocks and merely wants to make the buildings she constructs look more realistic, why not let her cut out logos from McDonald's, K-Mart, and other familiar names and tape them to the building-block buildings she's constructed? She can find plenty of golden arches and other familiar logos in the Sunday paper's advertising supplements, as well as on bags filled with fast food that find their way into your home, and ads that fill your mailbox.

The layout of Kiddie City can vary from one play session to the next. Chances are you don't have a permanent place for even a 4-by-5-foot city, and your child will have to take down the play city from one time to the next, reconstructing it every time she wants to play with it. Your junior city planner can improve on the layout with every new rebuilding. Does the park go alongside City Hall, alongside the school, or next to the skyscraper? Does the tall office building belong next to the firehouse? Where's a good place for Dairy Queen?

The tarp or other plastic that's the base of the city will probably be strong enough for your young urban planner to crawl around on, and probably be cheap enough that you can buy more than one, drawing a permanent lake on one, an unchange-able park on another, a golf course or other immovable, permanently drawn feature on a third. If you want, you can draw a straightforward city-blocks grid on the first tarp, a few curved roads on a subsequent tarp, and a hub-and-spokes arrangement à la Washington on yet another. Your child can not only reconstruct the city into an ever-better layout every time, she can take her choice of which basic plan to build on as well.

Spool Tool

Materials: To make the spool rack: one sheet of wood 1 by 8 inches or larger, and about 18 inches high (depending on the number of spools of thread you have), one finishing nail 1 1/2 to 2 inches long for each spool, hammer. To hang the spool rack, if desired: twine or picture-hanging wire, two eyebolts or nails to attach the wire to, one sturdy nail to pound into the wall and hang the wire on. To arrange thread: one spool rack and all the spools of thread you own.

Whether your child is going to make a spool rack for you or just organize the thread spools on the rack depends on his age. Is he old enough to use a hammer and nails responsibly? Great. He can make a spool rack for you. Not only will he be occupied for a while as he constructs the spool rack for you, you'll wind up with a genuinely useful piece of equipment.

Here's how to make a spool rack: Take a piece of wood (pine board is good for this) large enough to accommodate all the spools of thread on hand. Mark a spot every two or two-and-a-half inches across the board, repeating these spots all the way down the board.

Now drive a finishing nail into the board at each spot. (Finishing nails are the kind without a flaring head.) The nail should be driven in at about a 45 degree angle, so the spool won't slip off once it's hanging on the nail. Drive it in till about one-quarter of its length is into the wood, and the rest sticks out for the spool to slip over.

The spool board can rest on the floor, of course, but it can also be hung on the wall within easy reach of your sewing machine, if you have one, or close by wherever you usually sit when you sew by hand. Use an eyebolt or a nail in each of the two upper corners to hold a length of twine or picture-hanging wire. Drive a nail into the wall where you want the spool board to hang, and anchor the wire or twine over the nail.

Arranging the spools on the spool board is a fun project for the younger set. With a rainbow of threads to deal with, your young child can have fun arranging and rearranging the spools till he's found an arrangement that pleases his eye. Whatever arrangement he chooses, since the spools are out in plain sight, you'll have no trouble finding the color of thread you need for any given project, even if the colors aren't in an order you'd have chosen.

152

Grab-Bag Guessing Game

Materials: Large bag, blindfold, ten small objects (of a size that all ten can fit in the bag at once), paper and pen or pencil

Unlike most of the activities in this book, this one requires your participation. Prepare for the game by putting ten different objects in a large bag. They should all be objects your child is familiar with. Blindfold the child and ask her to put one hand in the bag.

Time the child, giving her five minutes to identify the objects she feels. As she identifies an object, write it down. When the five minutes are up (or sooner if she makes ten identifications in less than that time), remove the blindfold, dump the contents of the bag onto a table or other surface, and compare the list of items as she identified them with their actual identities.

Football-Card Football

Materials: Those football cards your child has all over his room—or baseball, hockey, or other sports cards

I've known adults to play this game, too, believe it or not, but it's easy enough for any child to play who's old enough to read the statistics on the back of the cards.

In this game, two teams face off against each other, each represented by one player whose card your child has. The two teams don't have to be this year's teams; your child can pit the 1956 Giants against the 1992 Dolphins.

Your child checks the statistics of the two players representing the two teams in the matchup, comparing the stats item by item. What is Player A's height? Player B's? The taller player scores a point for his team. Now compare weight, number of years on the team, age, even the player's number (the higher number wins)…each time one player outranks the other, he scores a point for his team.

As I said above, the same method works for other sports as well as for football. If your child is a baseball fanatic but doesn't care diddly for happenings on the gridiron, let him play baseball-card baseball (or, if hockey is his passion, then hockey-card hockey).

May the best team win!

Blockless Building

Materials: Empty boxes, cardboard paper towel or toilet paper tubes, overturned empty wastebaskets, books, small chair, and whatever else you see fit for your child to use

Just as switching from one set of building toys to another can be enough of a change to renew a bored child's interest in "construction," switching from a set of blocks or Legos to impromptu building materials can do the same. Who says you need a fancy, expensive set of blocks to build a building, a tower, a house, or similar construction?

What your child can use for alternative building materials is going to depend on what she has around, or what you have around, that's suitable. The items listed above are just suggestions and just a beginning. To that list, add such items as empty, rinsed-out plastic milk jugs, cardboard juice boxes, plastic glasses, and whatever else is lying around the house that won't break, won't hurt the child, and is in some reasonable proportion to the other materials she is assembling.

If you're not the kind of person who thinks using a book for anything but reading (or pressing flowers) is a desecration, she can (gently!) incorporate a book or two or more into the structure. If she has a small chair in her room, that can even be part of the building. Cardboard tubes from paper towels or toilet paper can serve as columns, spires, smokestacks, or chimneys.

Just mixing the materials together and coming up with a way to integrate them successfully will involve a certain degree of creativity and imagination. Creating a truly fine structure out of them all takes even more foresight and work.

Is your child tired of playing with her blocks or other building sets? Turn her loose with impromptu building materials and watch her get a fresh interest in becoming a junior engineer!

Ace of Towers
Materials: Old deck of cards you were going to throw out, scissors

Got a deck of cards with a bent 7 or missing 9? Don't throw it out. Give it to your child and turn him into a construction expert. Virtually every kid likes to be an engineer when it comes to towers, castles, and other buildings. And there are so many brands of commercial building blocks, logs, and other "construction materials."

What keeps the activity novel? Two things: One is trying to build new and different structures every time, the other is using different sets of blocks or logs instead of the same set every time.

Have I got a new set of construction materials for your child!

Give him that unusable deck of cards you were going to toss. No, I am not suggesting he build the traditional "house of cards," trying to balance one card on another on its side, unaided.

Not quite.

What I *am* suggesting is that *you* cut a half-inch-deep slit on each of the four sides of as many cards as you have the patience for. The slit should be right in the middle of each of the four sides (two long sides, two short ends). Now your child can interlock the cards...and make that tower of cards without it being at risk of toppling quite so easily.

He can join cards at their ends or at the sides, or join the end of one to the side of another. Because it's a new set of building tools, he'll be intrigued with them for a while even if he's tired of building with the construction sets he's already got. Too, the colorful cards provide an alternative to more prosaically colored construction sets.

The structures your child builds with cards won't look like realistic buildings, of course, but that's all the more opportunity for your child to use his imagination—a "muscle" I believe is sorely underdeveloped in too many kids today.

Hard hats in place, everyone. Building going up!

156 Splish-Splash Bowling

Materials: Balloons filled with water, small objects that can be bowled over by splashing water and won't be harmed by getting wet, such as empty pill bottles or lightweight toy soldiers or cowboys

Water balloons are fun on hot summer afternoons, but here's an activity that doesn't involve your child's wetting you, her friends, or the family dog. The child herself is likely to get splashed, but the main targets are small, lightweight toys or other objects small and light enough to be knocked over by water and made of material that won't be harmed by a good soaking.

The lightweight toys or other objects are the bowling "pins" your child will be aiming for, though the object isn't to knock them over with the balloons themselves, but rather with the water that will gush from the balloons.

There's no "right" way to set up the pins; they needn't be in the familiar, standard triangular arrangement found at the bowling alley. And there's no requirement that there be ten of them; if your child only has four toy figures the right size and weight, or six is all she can ever knock over at once, she can play with four, six, or any other number.

The procedure is for the child to aim the balloon near but not right at the set-up "pins." If the balloon itself knocks over the pins, the shot doesn't count. The pins must be knocked over by the force of the gushing water. Your child can lob the balloon from a short distance away, or she can drop the balloon next to the pins while standing directly above them. If she has yet another technique that works even better, let her use it. There is no correct way to propel the balloon; the rule is simply *not* to hit the pins with the balloon itself.

If your child wants to keep score, she can, but this is the kind of game that's usually best to play for the sheer fun of it, without scoring, without a whole lot of rules and do's and don'ts beyond what I've just laid out. Whether or not she even wants to follow the standard bowling rule of two balls—or in this case balloons—to knock down all the pins is entirely up to her.

A Button-Down Mind?
Materials: One button box full of buttons

An early comedy album of Bob Newhart's proclaimed his "button-down mind"—whatever that is. That doesn't imply that his mind is suited to sorting buttons, but I'll bet he enjoyed that activity as a child. Most kids do. In fact, there are a number of pastimes that can occupy a child who's turned loose with a button box that holds any appreciable assortment of buttons.

A child who's old enough to sew can take a sock, stuff about half of the foot portion of it with cotton, foam rubber from an about-to-be-discarded pillow, or whatever else you have that's suitable, put a rubber band below the stuffing, and sew buttons on the stuffed portion to create a rudimentary doll. Two big buttons form the eyes, a little button is the nose, and a row of buttons—at least four—placed so they touch (and, preferably, so that the line of them curls up at either end, forming a smile) creates the mouth. (If your child holds out for hair, too, use yarn and glue it on.)

But making a doll is far from the only thing that can be done with buttons.

How about a search through the button box for The World's Most Beautiful Button?

There are other quests that can be effected, too, and that subtly teach a child certain skills. Ask him to search for the largest button in the box, the smallest, the shiniest, the most colorful, the most unusual, and any other qualifier that suggests itself to you as you look over the treasure trove of playtime possibilities that, up till a few minutes ago, was a rather pedestrian assortment of fastener replacements and nothing more.

Then suggest your child sort the buttons.

The question is, how to sort them? There are lots of ways, all valid. He can sort them:

- By color
- By size
- By two-hole, four-hole, or shank
- By material: clearly plastic, ivory-looking, pearl-looking, gold-looking, silver-looking, fabric, and other

• In any other way that appeals to you or occurs to the child.

He can learn about groups and subgroups by sorting large from small, then two-hole, four-hole, and shank within each of the two larger groups, for instance.

Very young children can play "store" with buttons, using the buttons as money to buy pretend items.

Button-down mind? On the contrary, unbutton your mind and let your ideas flow, and you may think of countless more ways your child can have a good time with your button box!

To-Whit-To...Who?

Materials: Bird identification book, possibly binoculars, possibly bird feeder

What was that bird that called "To-whit-to-whoo"? And look over there...what's that colorful bird? It's blue, but is it a bluebird, a blue jay, or something else altogether?

If your child has a book on birds, she can identify them by either looks or calls. A good bird identification book can be purchased at most bookstores or borrowed from the library. Not sure whether your child is going to get seriously interested in bird-watching, be briefly caught up and then lose interest, or yawn from the minute you mention birds? Start with a library book, then buy one (or more) books if she shows a genuine interest.

The only equipment she really *needs* is a book on birds. Additional equipment that will be *helpful* includes binoculars, for seeing birds at long range, and a bird feeder for your backyard, for luring birds within viewing range. (She might also want a camera for taking pictures of birds, or, if she's talented at drawing, a paint set for painting pictures of birds.)

Sit! Heel! Roll Over!
Materials: One pet, possibly a book on pet training or obedience, treats to reward the pet with when it does tricks on command

The next time your child complains that there's no one to play with, if he has a pet, you might point out that though there's nobody *two-legged* to play with, he does have a pet…and now is as good a time as any to teach that pet some tricks.

Clearly I'm not talking about a goldfish. But dogs, some cats, and even birds can be taught many tricks with patience and the proper training. Whole books have been devoted to the subject of training animals, and certainly it's nothing I can get into in a brief space here, so if your child has never taught a pet a trick before, and you don't know how either, buy or borrow a book on the subject.

You'll need a supply of treats for rewarding the animal for performing properly. Now, following the book's instruction, your child can teach the animal to roll over, dance on its hind legs…or some "stupid pet trick" that could land it on Letterman.

Teaching an animal a trick is not a quick process. Your child shouldn't expect to accomplish it instantaneously. But he'll be able to take great pride in his accomplishment when Spot shows off a newfound ability to shake hands. And your child will glow with pride at his own accomplishment.

My Memory Book

Materials needed: White writing or typing paper, construction paper, hole punch, yarn, pen, crayons or paints, possibly photos and glue or paste

What's a memory book? It isn't a diary, it isn't a scrapbook, and it isn't a photo album, but it contains some elements of each. This particular type of memory book is a scrapbook in which your child will collect her favorite memories in words and pictures.

The first thing the child needs to do is make a list of her favorite memories. These can include special occasions such as birthdays, Christmases, trips to the fair and such, as well as special memories of more everyday occasions. Is there an airplane trip, first horseback ride, visit from a special aunt, visit from a friend who had moved away, or some other such occasion that your child remembers fondly? You can prompt and give hints, but let her be the final arbiter of which memories do and don't go into the book.

Most memory books celebrate happy occasions, but if your child chooses to include a sad memory, don't discourage her. The death of her pet gerbil, though sad, may be meaningful and emotion-laden. Don't dismiss or make light of the memory, or deem it unsuited for the book.

Now that she has a list, she should start writing out the story of each occasion. She can take as few or as many words to describe each memory as she wants, but each memory should go on one side only of a separate sheet of paper (or more than one sheet if needed). The reason for writing on only one side is so that your child can then paste or glue the white writing paper onto a sheet of construction paper. On another piece of construction paper your child can draw or paint a picture of the occasion, or some aspect of the occasion. If a memory takes more than one page to write about, she can draw a picture for each page she's written on.

An alternative to drawing pictures is to utilize spare family photos of the occasion, if you have them. You may not have photos for many of the memories, though. If one memory is of the day Bobby brought his new parakeet home from the store, it's very probable that nobody took pictures of the occasion. Of course, you might have a picture of the bird that was taken subsequently, but then again, you might not. And if one memory is of the time that Dad came home from Europe after a two-month business trip, it's probable that everyone was too busy hugging to take pictures. But where there are pictures in existence, your child may wish to use them to illustrate the book.

Now she needs to paint or crayon a cover page for the memory book—probably with a title such as *Bonnie's Memory Book* or *Bonnie's Best Memories* or some such, though she's free to be more creative if she wishes. The inside front cover can be left blank or decorated. The first page can contain an illustration, either drawn or painted right on the construction paper or drawn or painted on a piece of white paper that's then pasted or glued onto a piece of construction paper. Another option is to list a table of contents on a piece of white paper, pasting that onto a piece of construction paper.

The other side of that sheet of paper is page two of the book, and there your child should place the illustration for the first memory. Again, it can be drawn or painted directly on the construction paper or drawn on white typing paper and pasted onto the construction paper. On the facing page—page three— she pastes a sheet of white paper with the first memory written on it. If the memory takes more than one page to write, page four should be another illustration and page five the continuation of the story she's telling of the incident she remembers. As an alternative, if the continuation of the story takes two or more pages, she can paste them on pages four and five, omitting further illustrations.

She continues in that manner throughout the book.

What order she puts the memories in is entirely up to the child. They can be in chronological order, or grouped by classification (holiday and birthday memories together, summer camp memories together, school memories together, family memories together), or they can be in some other order that works for her, or even in random order.

163

In drawing and pasting, though, she should give thought to the fact that she's going to be punching two holes in the paper, and not write or draw where the holes are going to go.

Now about those holes…she needs to punch one hole perhaps three inches from the top of the paper, and another perhaps three inches from the bottom, on the left side of each odd-numbered page (which is, of course, the right side of the even-numbered pages). A piece of yarn through the holes will make a decorative fastener to hold the pages together.

The memory book doesn't have to be irrevocably finished when she's done making it. As more happy or meaningful occasions occur in her life, she can easily add them to the memory book by writing about them, drawing suitable pictures, and adding the pages to the book. (If she's got a table of contents on page three, she'll have to update it.)

A note: When your child reaches the "maturity" of adolescence, she might be embarrassed by the perceived silliness of some of the memories in the memory book. Encourage her to hold on to the book anyhow, through the emotional and easily embarrassed adolescent years. It will be very meaningful to her once she has reached the safety of adulthood.

Treasure Chest

Materials: Box, glue or paste, scissors, decorations such as one or more of the following: wallpaper scraps, leftover giftwrap, glitter imitation jewels (from crafts store), construction paper, yarn, shells, crayons or paints, cutout pictures from the comics, photos of the child, cutout sports photos from the newspaper or a magazine

Everybody has treasures, and what better place to keep them than in a treasure chest. Even if the family has a scrapbook in which they keep souvenirs from trips they took together and other momentous family occasions, your child surely has some items he's keeping that are precious to him but not to the family at large.

It could be something with no sentimental value that he simply treasures for its appearance, such as a particularly beautiful rock or shell he's found. It could be a softball he hit a homer with, or a baseball he caught on a trip to a major league stadium, one that was hit into the stands and landed in your child's lap. It might be an autographed celebrity photo, a school award, a letter from a friend who moved across the country, a prized football card, a valentine, or any other treasure. Chances are, your child has accumulated a number of such items he holds in great value. Why not one box to keep all these goodies in?

He needs to pick a sturdy box, large enough to hold all his current treasures with some room to grow into as more treasures are accumulated. Since a plain box isn't as satisfying as something more decorative and personalized, he'll want to decorate it. There are many ways to go about this.

Pictures of sports figures, pop singers, or other celebrity figures of interest can be cut out and glued to the box, either side-by-side or collage style. Favorite comic strip characters, either of the "action" type or funny or cute, can be similarly cut out and pasted onto the box. Or the child may want to decorate the box with pictures of himself. After all, it's his very own treasure chest.

165

Another means of decorating a treasure chest is with a piece of leftover wallpaper or wrapping paper, which can be glued onto the box, both lid and bottom, to cover it. Or the child can spell out his name in glue or paste on the boxtop, then sprinkle glitter over the boxtop. The glue will hold the glitter, which will spell out the child's name, and the rest of the glitter will fall off the boxtop when the top is held on its side and rapped sharply against a hard surface.

Or he can lay some yarn into that same glue that's been put down to spell out the child's name (preferably in script), and the glue will hold the yarn in place, spelling out the name.

Of course, the glitter or yarn can be used to spell out "Treasure Chest," to create a picture, or to otherwise decorate the boxtop.

Small shells from the shore or imitation jewels from a crafts store are other suitable decorations for a treasure chest.

Your child can also crayon or paint the box to decorate it. If the box is a dark color, or has writing on it, the child may want to cover it with construction paper first, then paint or crayon on the construction paper.

Be an Inventor
Materials: Paper and pen

Be an inventor and be a hero. If your child can invent a new game, a good game that the other kids will enjoy playing, they'll really appreciate him or her. After all, all games were made up by someone. From copyrighted boxed games like Monopoly and Scrabble to simple childhood games like London Bridge or even tag or hide-and-seek, *someone* had to think up the premise, the rules, and whatever other variables there are.

So the next time there's no one around to play with, instead of fretting or pouting, your child can utilize the downtime to think up a new game to play when there are other kids around again.

Presenting...Our New DJ!
Materials: Cassette recorder with mike (built-in or external), second cassette recorder or built-in second deck, blank cassette tape, cassette tapes with music on them

The above list of materials sounds more daunting than it is. Many kids these days get "boom boxes" at an early age, and many of these oversized portable cassette recorders have a built-in mike and two decks. Lacking a two-deck recorder, your child can use two one-deck recorders, even two little handheld recorders.

Placing the blank tape in the record deck, she loads a music tape in the other deck (or in the second recorder). She cues up the music tape till it's ready to play the first song she wants. Now she presses Record and speaks into the mike. She may want to start with a welcome to her "audience," and of course she'll want to say who she is. With perhaps a bit of patter as prelude, she announces the first song, presses Play on the second deck, and lets the song play through. She pushes the Pause button, cues up the next song, and then presses Record again and announces it, playing it immediately thereafter.

She can "program" a full tape of songs interspersed with her introductions and other patter, trying to sound as professional, as much like a real DJ as she can. She may wish to emulate her favorite DJ on the radio, or strike out and try for her own unique sound.

167

And Now This Public Service Message

Materials: Paper and pen, tape and tape recorder (see item above)

If your child enjoys putting together tapes of music interspersed with his voice doing the DJ chores, he may also enjoy writing public service announcements and recording them on the tape.

You know what PSAs are—they're the "noncommercial commercials" that tell you only you can prevent forest fires, or this is national safety week, or you should give to your community's current blood drive.

Your child can certainly think of a few appropriate messages to convey to the friends who may be listening to the tape he's putting together (see Presenting...Our New DJ! above). They may include an admonition not to litter the neighborhood, or a reminder to recycle and engage in other activities to keep our earth green.

First he needs to write the PSAs, then perhaps rehearse his delivery of them, depending how seriously he's taking being a DJ. Last, he needs to record them on the tape.

If he happens to be an enterprising young businessperson with a lemonade stand, comic books for sale, or baseball cards he's selling or trading, he could record a commercial or two, too.

"I Did Not Say 'Clean Your Room'"

Materials: One room in need of organizing

While *cleaning* her room is a dreaded activity for the average child, *organizing* that same room can be a downright pleasurable activity for a certain kind of child. And for the rest, if you point out that organizing her room will make it easier and less time-consuming to clean, you've got the incentive that will make the activity seem acceptable, reasonable, if not fun.

So what does organizing a room consist of? That depends on the child and the room. If the child has a lot of collections, a lot of things that need to be kept together (jacks, marbles, baseball cards, celebrity photos, or any other groups of small things), the first thing is to decide on suitable containers.

One solution is a shoe bag, the kind of thing that hangs up and has pockets in it for shoes. Only instead of putting pairs of shoes in the pockets, the child can keep jacks in this pocket, marbles in that pocket, baseball cards in this pocket, football cards in that pocket, pages of stickers or decals in another pocket, and so on. A label on each pocket will tell the child at a glance what's supposed to go in each pocket. (If you don't happen to have one of those label makers at home, you can improvise by writing on a little piece of paper and taping or pinning that paper onto each pocket of the shoe bag.)

The idea, though, is to *organize* the room so that there's a place for everything. Then, whether the problem is little things that belong in collections and need a home, or comic books that need to be kept in boxes, or some other type of organization, your child will have solved two problems at once. If your child will get her room in a sensible order, with each type of possession in its own place, in a place that is easily accessible for removal and return, she'll have made the room easier to clean and also have made it easier to find things in the future. ("Ma! I can't find my history notes! Mom! I can't find my doll clothes! Hey, has anyone seen my jigsaw pieces?")

But the first step is organizing. Some kids will really get into it: butterfly stickers in this drawer, smiley-face stickers in that drawer. Break down and classify, put away and catalog what went where. For the majority, it won't be that enjoyable an activity to get into, and they won't throw themselves into it with quite that fervor, but if they do get the place organized, the future rewards will more than pay off for the work involved.

A related activity worth mentioning here is arranging in order the child's books, cassette tapes, and conceivably videos or CDs if she has any that are considered her own. In the case of books, this can be alphabetical order by title or by author, organizing by subject, or any other classification that may come to mind and work for the child.

Rearrange Your Room

Materials: Paper and pen, measuring tape, child's room

Akin to organizing the child's room is rearranging it. Nearly everyone gets tired of his room's arrangement from time to time. Moreover, what worked two years ago doesn't work as well now.

The girl whose room's focus was a huge dollhouse two years ago may now have a big bookcase as the most important item in her room. The boy who now has a TV set and stereo in his room may no longer really need that oversized, space-consuming toy chest. Or perhaps a second bed was added for friends on sleep-overs.

Then again, maybe nothing was added or subtracted, but priorities have simply changed. A piece of furniture of less significance previously now needs to be more accessible, differently situated. The bed used to be up against the wall, taking less floor space and leaving more room for playing board games in the middle of the floor. Now your child is more into activities that require desk space rather than floor space. If you moved the bed so that only the head was up against the wall, you'd have room along the wall for the desk that's sitting in storage in the basement.

Whether you've got a husky twelve-year-old who can move his own furniture or a small eight-year-old who needs help with the physical rearranging, he should plan it out on paper first.

Your child (possibly with some input from you, depending on the child's age) needs to decide what arrangement of furniture would work best, be most pleasing, give the most sensible use of floor space, and whatever other considerations there are. He should plan it out on paper and make sure that it's going to work before anyone actually lugs heavy pieces of furniture needlessly.

("No. That doesn't work. And this doesn't fit. Put it back the way it was.") Then your child, you, or whoever is appropriate can actually move the furniture.

So let your child spend some time in his room with a pencil and some paper and a measuring tape. Let him make a drawing, or several, of the best way to rearrange his furniture. When he's come up with the plan that suits him best, and works on paper complete with measurements, you can tackle the job of actually moving the furniture.

And, for a while after the rearrangement is complete, your child may be so happy with the new look of the room, and the more workable arrangement, that he may even keep his room cleaner and neater. For a while. Maybe.

Snow Paintings

Materials: Preferably at least four spray bottles, food coloring (all four standard colors), water, snow on the ground

When most kids think of "decorating" fresh snow, they think in terms of "snow angels," made by lying in the snow and moving their arms and legs. It's fun to do, but a child can get awfully wet and cold that way. Snow paintings require no contact, no getting cold and wet. All they require is the items above and a trigger finger.

Put some water and a few drops of food coloring in each spray bottle. You can make do with just one bottle, one color, of course, and paint the snow red (or blue, green, or yellow). But with one of each of all four basic food colors, your child can be a cold-weather Rembrandt. And if you happen to have lots of spray bottles around, your child can mix colors, dilute colors, and come up with both red and pink, dark blue and light, as well as orange, aqua, purple, and other, even more exotic hues.

It's preferable if your spray bottles shoot a fine stream, rather than a dissipated mist.

The child can write her name, draw pictures, even paint elaborate scenery. How about some swaying palm trees under a brilliant orange sun, to give a little pictorial relief to the unrelenting real-life winterscape?

You may wind up with the most unusual front yard in town this winter!

Pinfinders, Inc.

Materials: As many clothespins as there are rooms in your home. (In lieu of clothespins, see below for suggestions of other items you can substitute.)

With only a minimal amount of preparation on your part, you can keep your restless little one occupied for quite a nice long while with this game. Your part in this enterprise: Hide one clothespin in each room of your home. His part: Find it.

Obviously you want to hide each clothespin someplace where the child isn't going to find it thirty seconds after entering the room, but on the other hand, you don't want to place any of the pins in sites so obscure that the child will hunt for twenty minutes, get frustrated, and start whining. (Is there anything worse to listen to than a whining child? My only candidate for worse-than-whining is a phonograph record—remember those?—with a nick in it, causing the needle to get stuck and play "Twinkle, twinkle, little star, star, star, star, star, star...")

Depending on your child's age, any hazards in your house, and any privacy requirements of other family members, you may have to set up ground rules such as, "There's nothing hidden in your sister's dresser, on any high closet shelves, or in Dad's workshop."

It's not unreasonable to offer a modest reward—a candy bar or a cup of frozen yogurt—if the child finds all the clothespins. But not all kids need the incentive of a tangible reward; for many, the pleasure of being victorious will be reward enough.

One nice thing about this game is that each room feels to the child like a fresh, new challenge. There's no sense of doing the same thing over and over. The new site makes it feel like a new game, and the child won't grow tired of playing before he's found all the pins...unless you hide one in so good a hiding spot that he simply can't find it at all. And each challenge—each room, that is—offers a sense of reward right on the spot, when the child finds the pin that's hidden there.

As your child plays the game more and more often, you'll need to think of new, different places in which to hide the clothespins. And as he gets more adept at the game, you'll need to find ever more challenging spots in which to hide them.

If you don't have clothespins in the house and don't feel like going out and buying them just for the game, other items can be substituted. Index cards are a possibility, as are the plastic cases from cassette tapes. (I don't know what you do with the cases from tapes that have gotten unfixably eaten by a tape deck or otherwise messed up, but I have a humongous stack of empties that I'm saving—heaven knows why.) The little gray-and-black containers that film comes in are another good item to substitute for clothespins, as are empty pill bottles, or the caps from plastic milk or juice jugs.

Variation—Spell Me a Treat

This switch on Pathfinders, Inc., involves the same activity as above, but with some variations. First of all, the clothespins, bottle caps, or whatever you hide need to have letters on them—letters spelling out the treat you plan to reward your child with if he finds all the pins. So you first have to write one letter on each pin, cap, etc., before hiding it. If the treat is a candy bar, for example, you'll need eight pins—regardless of the number of rooms in your house—one pin for each of the eight letters in "candy bar."

Write one letter on each pin, then hide the pins in the various rooms of the house. (Or hide them all in one room, for this game, if you prefer.) If you're hiding them in different rooms, as in the basic game, you'll need to tell your child which rooms have no pins in them, or which rooms have more than one pin in them, unless you have exactly the same number of rooms in your house as there are letters in the treat.

When your child has found all eight pins (or twelve if the treat is an ice cream cone, or seven if the treat is raisins—you get the idea), he still isn't finished. Now he has to arrange the pins in order to spell out the treat. Until he's unscrambled the letters, he doesn't get the treat. (For a long word or a multiword phrase, such as "ice cream cone," you may have to give some clues or break the pins down into piles, one pile for each word in the treat: "ice," "cream," and "cone.")

If you're teaching your child a foreign language, or his school is, you can make the letters spell out a treat in the language your child is studying. If rearranging the letters is too easy for your child and not enough of a challenge, and he doesn't speak a foreign language, you can utilize a simple code (see Secret Codes, page 26) and require the child to break the code before he can collect the reward.

Your ingenuity and your child's age and ability are the only boundaries to what kind of clues you can present him with.

The Price Is Right—Right at Home

Materials: Pen, small stickers

Another activity that involves your participation, this one calls for you to provide a packet of peel-off labels and a pen for your child. The little round labels are good for this, though by no means the only kind that work. When you offer her these labels, you're also offering a chance for your child to get a better concept of what things cost.

Have you ever had your child put a nick in an antique table or break an expensive plate, then have her smile disarmingly and offer, "You can keep my next week's allowance to pay for it"? This game will teach her that 75¢ won't cover the cost of a broken footstool, and why she should treat that set of encyclopedias with respect.

This isn't a game with a winner. Your child should be praised if she comes at all close in her guesses of what the various items are worth, but don't laugh when she prices a VCR at $2.59.

What you're asking her to do is guess the price of every item in the living room, family room, or den—wherever you choose—and write each guess on a sticker, affixing the sticker to the item in question.

Or, as an alternative, *you* choose the items you want her to guess at, and you affix stickers to those items. Then the child goes around the house, searching out the stickers, and writes her best guess at price on each of the stickers.

If the child is the one affixing the stickers, you need to be sure in advance to tell her if there are any items you don't want stickers on (such as furniture from which the adhesive will not easily come off, or any other possession that might be harmed by a sticker).

In the course of this game, she will learn—if she doesn't know already—that size is not a determinant of price. A small porcelain figure might be worth a great deal more than a large table, a rack of encyclopedias more than a sofa, and a VCR more than an end table, even though it would fit in the end table drawer.

So the game does more than merely keep a child occupied. It offers a chance to learn a very worthwhile lesson about the monetary value of items around the house—and one more reason to treat these belongings with respect.

Good Luck!

Materials: A yard during late spring, summer, or early Fall, and a nonrainy day

When's the last time you hunted for four-leaf clovers? Has your child *ever* hunted for them? It's never too late to start!

Actually, he'll have good luck even if he doesn't find what he's ostensibly after…he'll have the pleasure of crawling around in the grass, smelling fresh earth and sweet clover, watching ants and honeybees and butterflies, feeling the warm sun if it's not a cloudy day, possibly observing the difference between unob-structed, industrial-strength sunlight and the rays as they feel when diffused by shining through the umbrella of a live oak. How lucky can you get?

If your child does actually find a lucky clover, fold a piece of waxed paper or plastic wrap and put the four-leaf clover flat between the folded pieces. Then press the clover flat in the middle of the pages of a big, heavy book.

Forget about it...maybe even for a few years. When you come upon the four-leaf clover in future time, take it out, treasure it, and reflect back on all the good luck you and your child have had in the time since he first found it. Coincidence? Probably, but who knows?

Play the Waterphone

Materials: Eight glasses or jars, water, fork

As you are probably aware, a glass with a few drops of water in it makes a very different musical note when struck with a fork than does a glass that's nearly full. And different water levels between empty and full produce all different sounds up and down the musical scale.

If your child chooses, she can painstakingly add water bit by bit to each of eight glasses till she can perfectly reproduce the notes up the musical scale—*do, re, mi, fa, sol, la, ti, do*—by striking each glass lightly with a fork. If she's less of a perfectionist, she can simply fill eight glasses (or any other number) with varying amounts of water. Here, too, she'll get different notes with the fork, but she won't be able to play the scales.

If she has accomplished giving herself a perfect scale, she can now learn by trial and error how to play simple tunes. Any tune that doesn't involve sharps and flats or more than one octave is fair game. Some such simple tunes include "*Twinkle, Twinkle*," "*Jingle Bells*," and "*Happy Birthday to You.*"

Even if she hasn't re-created the eight notes of the scale, your child can have a good time playing around with the different glasses or jars, striking them to get different notes, making up tunes. And if your child has re-created *do* through *do* she can also make up her own tunes.

For those who have re-created the eight notes of the scale and are learning to play songs on the glasses or jars, it might be useful to label the glasses, either 1 through 8 or *do* through *do*, and write down the notes as she figures them out, so she'll have rudimentary "sheet music" from which to play the glasses in the future. Similarly, if she makes up a tune of her own, she may want to write down the notes of the tune so that she can play it at a later date. She can use a small piece of paper lightly taped to the glass, or a small press-on label.

Another piece of tape on each glass, right at the water level, will show her where to fill the glasses up to the next time she wants to play the waterphone, so all the trial-and-error of figuring it out won't be necessary.

Sock It to Me!

Materials: Clean socks on laundry day

Turn a chore from a bore to an activity that will have your child yelling "More!"

Got a basketful of socks to sort? Get your child to help sort them—the exercise in sorting, matching like with like, will be good for him—and then let him play "basketball" with the socks, aiming them at the appropriate drawers.

But sorting comes first. To you it's a dreaded chore, and to your child it may be, too, but to many kids it's an amusing activity, especially those still young enough to be into helping Mommy. Which sock goes with which? Is this one black or deep brown? Black or navy blue? Is this white sock a match with this one...or with the thinner one over here?

179

When the socks are all mated, there's the matter of rolling, an exercise in manual dexterity. And then comes the *really* fun part.

There's no harm in having a little fun while you're getting work done. The Seven Dwarfs knew enough to whistle while they worked. Whistling does make the work go faster. And what better excuse to whistle than because you're having fun? Fun makes work go faster too.

So have a little fun with the socks. Play basketball with them. With the appropriate drawers open, your child can lob pair after pair into his own drawer, any siblings' drawers, and the appropriate parental drawers. Standing at a suitable distance (to be determined by you), how many socks can he land in the drawer? In the right part of the drawer? In the right person's drawer?

Make sure he keeps a record of his score. He needs to know what this week's score was when he attempts to beat his own record next week on laundry day.

And Now a Word *About* Our Sponsor
Materials: Pen and paper, TV

We all despair at the reactions of kids who, on seeing a particular toy, cereal, sneaker, or other product advertised on TV, begin begging, pleading, whining, and making general nuisances of themselves because they absolutely *have* to have the item in question, pleasemompleasemompleasepleaseplease. Maybe if the kids knew just in what ways Madison Avenue works on them, they wouldn't be quite so manipulatable.

So the next time your child has no one to play with and turns the TV on out of boredom, how about saying, "Okay. You may watch TV. But I want you to pay close attention to the commercials...and write a report."

A report? Yes! Ask your child to write a report on three commercials, including answering the following questions:

- How do they make the product seem more appealing?
- What are they actually claiming about the product's qualities?
- Are their claims fair?
- Are their claims straightforward?
- What are their hidden messages?

If your child is too young to understand all of the questions above, ask fewer and simpler questions. The idea is to get her *thinking* about a commercial's purpose, its claims, and its methods of appealing to young consumers. If she's too young to ask all the above questions, that's okay. Any progress you make will be a help.

If she doesn't understand about hidden messages, use this example: Do they show a child or other person eating/wearing/using/playing with the product, and then excelling at something—such as wearing a particular sneaker and playing a great game of basketball, or owning a particular brand of doll and having three friends over, or eating a certain brand of cereal and standing up to bullies? The implication is that these sneakers will help you be great at sports, this doll will make you popular, this cereal will make you strong.

Now ask your child if she thinks a certain brand of cereal can really make her so strong that no one can beat her up, if a certain brand of sneaker can really make her a star athlete, if a particular toy will really suddenly make her popular (and if it does, are those the kind of friends she really wants—friends who like her only for the toys she has?).

Depending on the age of your child, your questions may be exactly those above, or you may ask fewer or simpler questions—or more questions and more thought-provoking ones. The idea is to make her aware of the forces at work on kids (and the rest of us) when they (and we) watch commercials.

I'm not promising that these questions will confer total immunity from manipulation—you and I both know better—but they will inoculate your child against a complete takeover of her brain and sales resistance by the whizzes of the ad world. And if you only hear "Mommy, buy me ___" half as often, if

181

your child is on the way to becoming an educated consumer and if your child learns to recognize some of the tricks of persuasion, isn't that half the battle?

Rock Face Paperweights
Materials: Smooth, flat rock, yarn (yellow, brown, black, or red), paint, small paintbrush, glue

Want your papers held down from breezes with a smile? Then ask your child to make you a rock face paperweight! And while he's at it, he can make one for Grandma, one for himself, and a few for other relatives and friends.

Here's how: Start with a smooth, flat rock. Paint a face on the top, preferably one that's smiling. Now cut five or six pieces of yarn of a suitable length that, when glued across the top, will drape on either side to look like hair—short or long, your choice.

Voilà! You've got a rock face paperweight, keeping your papers in place as it smiles up at you. How many of us smile so consistently as we do our jobs?

Work Plans
Materials: Paper and pen or pencil

Sometimes the task of cleaning her room (or the kitchen, the bathroom, the family room, or wherever) seems daunting to a child simply because the prospect seems overwhelming. The groan that such a request elicits arises not only because kids have an aversion to cleaning or an antipathy to orderly rooms but because *they just don't know where to start.*

What I'm suggesting is a work plan—a plan of action that can be written up even on a day when your child isn't expected to do a room-clean.

Sample scenario:

YOUR CHILD

"Mom! I'm bored. No one's around to play with."

YOU

"You know you're going to have to clean your room tomorrow."

CHILD

Groan

YOU

"If you've got nothing to do today, why don't you clean your room today and you won't have to deal with it tomorrow." **183**

CHILD

Louder groan

YOU

"Okay. How's this? Go into your room and make a plan. Figure out just what needs to be done. Figure out in what order you need to do things. Write everything down in the order you need to do it. Then tomorrow when you have to clean, it'll go much faster because you won't be standing there overwhelmed by the mess. You'll have a game plan."

CHILD

Small token groan

But off she goes and writes a plan:

Make bed

Put away clean laundry

Put dirty laundry in hamper

Put away books

Put away dolls

Clear mess from corner near window

Straighten dresser top, clear off

Dust room

Vacuum

Or whatever is appropriate to the mess in your child's particular room and to her age and the participation required of her. Maybe you don't ask her to dust and vacuum. Maybe there are many different kinds of things in a mess on the floor, and the list is more appropriately:

184

Clear all books off table and bed and put in bookcase

Put away all cassette tapes

All dirty laundry into laundry bag

Put away all toy cowboys in their box

All toy cars and trucks into their box

All Ninja stuff into their container

All miscellaneous and large toys into toy chest

The point is for her to go into the room, look around, and *with no thought of doing the work today*, make a complete list of everything that needs to be done, and in logical order.

Then tomorrow she'll have a plan of action and not be so overwhelmed by the mess that she's paralyzed and doesn't know where to start.

And, of course, it's also given her something to do *today* while there's no one to play with.

Birthday Calendar
Materials: Calendar, pen or pencil

How do *you* remember the birthdays of friends and family members? Chances are you have them written down somewhere, either in a birthday book, on a calendar, or in your appointment book.

Your children's friends have birthdays too. Wouldn't it be nice if your kids remembered their friends' birthdays even when there *isn't* a party? And shouldn't they remember the birthdays of Grandma and Grandpa, and all the rest of the family?

If your child already has a calendar of his own on the wall (marked with school closings, family vacations, the first day of camp, and such), fine. If not, now's the time to get one. (You don't have to buy a calendar—your insurance company, drugstore, or some other merchant or businessperson surely has a calendar left over from the first of the year and will have an extra one for you next year.)

Have your child label all the dates of his friends' birthdays, while you fill in relatives' birthdays (and any anniversaries or other special occasions you'd like your child to recognize with a card). If your child doesn't know all his friends' birthdays, he can ask them.

Get him in the habit of checking the calendar every weekend for special card-sending occasions coming up in the next two weeks. Then he can buy or make a card to send whenever it's appropriate.

This activity teaches both social responsibility and organization.

Paper Dolls

Materials: Paper, scissors, crayons or colored markers, optional: removable adhesive tape

Whatever happened to old-fashioned paper dolls? Some kids today still create and play with them; though paper dolls may be a dying art, the art's not dead yet. And they're simple enough to make.

Your child can make several different dolls with distinct personalities and looks: perhaps a blonde with curly hair, a redhead with striking short hair, a brunette with long, flowing tresses, and whatever other looks seem appealing. (Dolls can be male, too; after all, Barbie has her Ken.)

She can invest the dolls with personalities and backgrounds, then make the hair and makeup look as she'd imagine that person would. One can be a housewife and part-time real estate agent, another might be a nurse, another a high-powered business executive, another a retired grandma, another a secretary, another a farm wife...or choose other types.

These dolls should first be drawn and colored in on stiff paper (or cardboard), then cut out. If she wants them to stand up, she can glue a flap to the back of each doll that's nearly as wide as the doll itself and about half the doll's length, with a flat bottom that will perch on a flat surface (floor or tabletop).

She should attach the top of the flap at a point on the doll's back that will allow the base to rest on a table or wherever she's playing, just behind the doll's feet, allowing the doll to be nearly upright. But it isn't necessary to put such a flap on if she's content for the doll to stay lying down at any time she's not holding it.

Now the dolls need clothes. These are made of more lightweight paper, and can be attached to and removed from the dolls in several ways. The old-fashioned method is to include several flaps of paper that extend from the clothing at various points around the clothing. The flaps are folded around behind the doll. Admittedly not very securely, they do manage to hold the clothes on the dolls.

A more modern invention is removable cellophane tape. By folding a piece of this tape over so it forms a loop and adheres to itself, you can create the equivalent of double-faced removable tape, with which your child can hold the clothing on the doll. (There is, of course, ready-to-use double-faced tape, but it is not removable and most households don't happen to have a roll of it lying around, while there's an excellent chance you already have a roll of removable tape in the house.)

187

The dolls' wardrobes can include not only clothing but also shoes, hats, and such accessories as pocketbooks, scarves, and even jewelry. Paper dolls have traditionally been dress-up dolls, with the emphasis in play being primarily on clothing, rather than on pretend play. But who's to say your child can't play house, work, or school with them, if she wants.

Cardboard Dollhouses

Materials: Cardboard box (shoebox or larger, up to large carton), loose pieces of cardboard or tagboard, tape, crayons or paints, possibly paper and glue or paste

Though commercially manufactured dollhouses may be more finished-looking, more realistic, and sturdier, you can't deny the pure fun involved for a child in making a dollhouse herself. Not only is making the house as much fun as playing with it, but in creating it herself, she can set it up most any way she wants it. Does she want more or fewer bedrooms? A den? An eat-in kitchen or not? A one- or two-story house? She's the architect! (And these days, when more women are architects than in my childhood, it's not so improbable to think that building a dollhouse today could lead to an interest in architecture and a great career.)

Your child can color the outside of the box to her specifications, or she can leave it as is and just pretend. If the box or carton is plain on the outside, she can draw windows, a door or two, even a chimney if she wants, or even color in individual bricks if she really wants to take time with the project. She can paint the whole house, making it an attractive shade, perhaps a soft blue. She can crayon or paint bushes at ground level, representing landscaping against the front of the house.

If the carton has printing on it, and she wants to go for a realistic look on the outside, she can cover the outside with paper (white construction paper is a good choice), gluing or pasting it in place, then crayon or paint the windows, doors, and so forth on the paper. Or she can use a soft blue or gray, or some

188

other appropriate color of construction paper, representing the color the house is painted. A heavier grade of white typing paper, or even brown wrapping paper, will work too.

Assuming it's a two-story house, she'll need to create a floor. That's where the cardboard comes in. Taping several pieces of cardboard end to end, in the case of a large carton dollhouse, or cutting it to fit, in the case of a shoebox dollhouse, she tapes the cardboard in place to form a floor. More cardboard pieces form the walls.

If she wants to draw pictures on the walls, color them with crayons or paint, or add other more realistic touches to them, she needs to do this before taping the cardboard in place. The same applies to drawing windows on the walls of the box itself, which would be the exterior walls of the house. These need to be drawn in before the floor and walls are added.

An option to drawing in windows, pictures on the wall, or drapes is to cut pictures of these items from magazines and tape or glue them in place. It's a bit tricky, as there may not be enough windows of the right size to put throughout the house, but if your child has patience, she can certainly search through magazines and try to find what she needs. Pictures on the wall can be literally pictures of pictures, complete with frames, or she may find a pretty scene in a small picture—or even a part of a picture—in a magazine, and paste it to a wall with a brown construction-paper frame around it.

Furniture can be cut out of cardboard and colored, if she wants to stick to do-it-yourself instead of buying dollhouse furniture at a store. Rugs can be crocheted or knit from wool, or you may have carpet scraps or fabric scraps around that your child can use. Fabric scraps can also serve as drapes, blankets or sheets, or slipcovers.

If your child has small dolls the right size for the house, great! If not, she can create a doll family out of paper or cardboard.

Quickies

Materials: Vary with the activities; see each

Here are a few quick ideas for solo activities:

- For the better-than-novice basketball player with a hoop in his yard or driveway: Practice trick basketball shots—with eyes closed, with your back to the hoop, and any other shot you can think of.
- For the jacks player: Invent a new fancy. Practice it and get good at it before trying it out with friends.
- For the child who lives within walking distance of a park: Go fly a kite.
- For the child with a large enough yard to run in, or a house that you can run around: Run laps whenever there's no one to play with. Time yourself each time. Try to always improve your personal best.
- For the child who lives near a public racquetball court, public tennis practice backboard, abandoned house or other building that's safe to be around, or other large wall with no windows in danger of breaking: Pitch a tennis ball against the wall, aiming for a specified area and giving yourself a point every time you hit within that area.